JOSEF MENGELE THE ANGEL OF DEATH

The Horrific Story Of The Evil Nazis Doctor Who Carried Out The Experiment Of The Twins Of Auschwitz

Louis Luther

Table of Contents

CHAPTER ONE 3
    INTRODUCTION 3
CHAPTER TWO 5
    JOSEF MENGELE 5
CHAPTER THREE 8
    THE NAZI EXPERIMENT 8
CHAPTER FOUR 11
    THE TWIN EXAMINATION 11
CHAPTER FIVE 17
    CONCLUSION 17
    THE END 26

CHAPTER ONE

INTRODUCTION

On May 24, 1943, the killing camp at Auschwitz, Poland, gets another specialist, 32-year-old Josef Mengele, a man who will procure the epithet "the Angel of Death."

Conceived March 16, 1911, in Bavaria, Mengele considered way of thinking under Alfred Rosenberg, whose racial hypotheses exceptionally affected him. In 1934, effectively an individual from the Nazi Party, he joined the examination staff of the

Institute for Hereditary Biology and Racial Hygiene.

CHAPTER TWO

JOSEF MENGELE

After showing up at Auschwitz, and anxious to propel his clinical profession by distributing "weighty" work, he started probing live Jewish detainees. In the appearance of clinical "treatment," he infused, or requested others to infuse, a huge number of prisoners including petroleum to chloroform. He additionally had an affinity for examining twins, whom he used to dismember.

Mengele figured out how to get away from detainment after the war, first by filling in as a ranch stableman in Bavaria, at that point by advancing toward South America. He turned into a resident of Paraguay in 1959. He later moved to Brazil, where he got together with another previous Nazi gathering part, Wolfgang Gerhard. In 1985, a worldwide group of scientific specialists ventured out to Brazil looking for Mengele. They verified that a man named Gerhard, however accepted to be Mengele, had kicked the bucket of a stroke while swimming in 1979. Dental records later affirmed that Mengele had, eventually, accepted that Gerhard's personality, and was in truth the stroke casualty.

Driven by doctor Josef Mengele, the program transformed twins like Eva and Miriam into reluctant clinical subjects in tests that uncovered around 3,000 kids at Auschwitz-Birkenau to ailment, distortion and torment under the pretense of clinical "research" into disease, human perseverance and the sky is the limit from there.

CHAPTER THREE

THE NAZI EXPERIMENT

Twins were isolated from different detainees during the enormous "determinations" that occurred at the camp's huge train stage, and sped off to a research center to be analyzed. Mengele normally utilized one twin as a control and oppressed the other to everything from blood bondings to constrained insemination, infusions with illnesses, removals, and murder. Those that passed on were analyzed and examined; their enduring twins were murdered and exposed to a similar investigation.

Twin investigations had helped researchers like Mengele's coach legitimize what they saw as fundamental victimization individuals with "unfortunate" hereditary attributes—Jews, Roma individuals, LGBTQ individuals, individuals with handicaps and others. However, the twin investigations that had made the selective breeding development would, unexpectedly, lead to the defeat of genetic counseling itself.

For eugenicists like Mengele, indistinguishable twins like the Mozes sisters were the ideal examination subjects. Since they share a genome, researchers contemplated, any physical or social contrasts in twins would be because of conduct, not hereditary qualities. Eugenicists considered hereditary qualities liable for bothersome attributes and social conditions like culpability and neediness. They accepted that particular rearing could be utilized to support socially satisfactory conduct and crash bothersome propensities.

CHAPTER FOUR

THE TWIN EXAMINATION

When twin examination started at Auschwitz-Birkenau during the 1940s, the utilization of twins in logical experimentation was many years old. In spite of the fact that earlier twin examinations had delivered developing proof that climate was as significant as hereditary qualities, genetic counseling specialists clung to the possibility that they could open new experiences into nature and support through contemplating them.

One of them, Otmar von Verschuer, had huge force and impact in Nazi Germany. He composed writings that affected Nazi arrangements toward Jews, Roma individuals and others, contending that race had an organic premise and that "mediocre" individuals could spoil the Aryan race. A supporter for constrained cleansing and particular rearing, von Verschuer gathered hereditary data on huge quantities of twins, considering the measurements trying to decide if everything from ailment to criminal conduct could be acquired. Furthermore, he had a protege: a youthful doctor named Josef Mengele.

Like his coach, Mengele was eagerly bigoted and a gave individual from the Nazi Party. In 1943, he started working at Auschwitz-Birkenau as a clinical official. From the start, Mengele was accountable for the Roma camp there, however in 1944 the whole residual populace of the camp was killed in the gas chambers. Mengele was elevated to boss camp doctor of the whole Birkenau camp, and got known for his severe determinations of approaching detainees for the gas chambers. Mengele needed to proceed with the twin examinations he had started with von Verschuer, and now he had a hostage people on which to do as such. Despite the fact that his prior examinations had been authentic, his work in Auschwitz-Birkenau was definitely not. Forsaking clinical morals and exploration conventions, Mengele started directing awful analyses on up to 1,500 arrangements of twins, a significant number of them youngsters. The "Mengele Twins" got ostensible assurance from a portion of the attacks of life at Auschwitz-Birkenau. They were not chosen for the gas chambers, lived in independent quarters, and were given extra food and clinical consideration. In return, however, they turned into the reluctant subjects of heartless tests because of Mengele, who increased a notoriety for being the "Holy messenger of Death" for his capacity, his inconsistent temper and his brutality.

For Eva, life as a Mengele twin implied sitting bare for quite a long time and having her body more than once estimated and contrasted with Miriam's. She withstood infusions of an obscure substance that caused extreme responses. "As twins, I realized that we were special since we were never allowed to communicate with anyone in different pieces of the camp," she later reviewed. "In any case, I didn't realize I was being utilized in hereditary examinations."

CHAPTER FIVE

CONCLUSION

Selective breeding itself was established in twin examination. Frances Galton, a British researcher who instituted the expression "genetic counseling" in 1883, had utilized twin examinations in his soonest eugenic exploration. For Galton and different selective breeding scientists, twins held the way to understanding which qualities were hereditary and which ones were natural. Utilizing information gathered through self-announced surveys, Galton contemplated many sets of twins to decide how they were comparable and unique. He reasoned that likenesses between twins were because of their hereditary qualities. "The one component that changes in various people, yet is steady in every one of them, is the common propensity," he composed. "It definitely stands up for itself."

In spite of the fact that Galton's twin exploration was one-sided and truly imperfect by current guidelines, it helped establish the framework for the selective breeding development. It additionally persuaded different eugenicists that twins were the ideal method to examine nature and sustain. In any case, however eugenicists theorized that twins could assist them with making more immaculate people, the consequences of twin investigations continued bewildering researchers. During the 1930s, for instance, a gathering of American specialists who thought about twins found a huge fluctuation in IQ in twins who had been raised separated yet regardless had comparative characters and social attributes.

Despite the fact that twins were "the most good weapons" for the investigation of the "much-discussed nature-sustain issue," they composed, their decisions recommended that the very characteristics eugenicists figured they could empower by checking marriage and wiping out people with "unfortunate" qualities from the genetic supply didn't have to do with hereditary qualities by any means.

The Nazis' annihilation finished Mengele's experimentation on twins at Auschwitz. Toward the finish of the war, the "Blessed messenger of Death" figured out how to get away from indictment. Protected by Nazi supporters, he lived in South America until his demise in Brazil in 1979.

In the result of the war, researchers wrestled with the fallout of Nazi experimentation and the Holocaust's utilization of eugenic standards for the sake of massacre. In 1946, a gathering of German doctors who had completed killing and led clinical experimentation in Nazi concentration camps were attempted at Nuremberg during a 140-day-long preliminary. The preliminary brought about seven capital punishments and the Nuremberg Code, a lot of exploration morals that has affected present day ideas of educated assent and clinical experimentation.

Just 200 of the 3,000 twins exposed to clinical trials at Auschwitz endure. Among them were Eva and Miriam. During the 1970s, Eva Mozes Kor started addressing about her encounters and searching out different survivors. Inevitably, she and Miriam framed a charitable called

Children of Auschwitz Nazi Deadly Lab Experiments Survivors (CANDLES) and found in excess of 100 other twin survivors, recording their encounters and the wellbeing implications of the frequently obscure tests they had been exposed to at Auschwitz.

Most records of experimentation at Auschwitz were crushed, yet the lives of individuals like Eva Mozes Kor, who passed on in July 2019 at age 85, give testimony regarding the twin examinations' fierceness. Incidentally, the very sort of experimentation Nazi doctors thought would maintain the pseudoscience they used to legitimize destruction wound up sabotaging the field of genetic counseling. Even with unconvincing information uncovered by twin investigations and overall judgment of Nazi clinical analyses, researchers relinquished selective breeding as a group and the field vanished.

At the point when war ejected, Mengele was a clinical official with the SS, the first class crew of Hitler's guardians who later developed as a mystery police power that pursued missions of dread for the sake of Nazism. In 1943, Mengele was called to a place that would gain him his merited ignominy. SS head Heinrich Himmler designated Mengele the main specialist of the Auschwitz concentration camps in Poland.

THE END

Printed in Great Britain
by Amazon

Mindfulness

Top 10 Tips to Overcoming Obsessions and Compulsions Using Mindfulness

Charlie Mason

Charlie Mason

© Copyright 2017 by Charlie Mason - All rights reserved.

The following eBook is reproduced below with the goal of providing information that is as accurate and as reliable as possible. Regardless, purchasing this eBook can be seen as consent to the fact that both the publisher and the author of this book are in no way experts on the topics discussed within, and that any recommendations or suggestions made herein are for entertainment purposes only. Professionals should be consulted as needed before undertaking any of the action endorsed herein.

This declaration is deemed fair and valid by both the American Bar Association and the Committee of Publishers Association and is legally binding throughout the United States.

Furthermore, the transmission, duplication or reproduction of any of the following work, including precise information, will be considered an illegal act, irrespective whether it is done electronically or in print. The legality extends to creating a secondary or tertiary copy of the work or a recorded copy and is only allowed with an express written consent of the Publisher. All additional rights are reserved.

The information in the following pages is broadly considered to be a truthful and accurate account of facts, and as such any inattention, use or misuse of the information in question by the reader will render any resulting actions solely under their purview. There are no scenarios in which the publisher or the original author of this work can be in any fashion deemed liable for any hardship or damages that may befall them after undertaking information described herein.

Additionally, the information found on the following pages is intended for informational purposes only and should thus be considered, universal. As befitting its nature, the information presented is without assurance regarding its continued validity or interim quality. Trademarks that mentioned are done without written consent and can in no way be considered an endorsement from the trademark holder.

CONTENTS

	Introduction	4
1	What Is OCD?	Pg 5
2	Deep Breathing	Pg 7
3	Take Notice of Your Surroundings	Pg 9
4	Slow Down	Pg 11
5	Meditate	Pg 13
6	Develop Concentration	Pg 15
7	Be Kind to Yourself	Pg 17
8	Journaling	Pg 19
9	Counseling	Pg 21
10	Don't Be Judgmental	Pg 23
11	Let Go And Have Fun	Pg 25
	Conclusion	Pg 27

INTRODUCTION

Twenty years ago, the idea of being mindful was largely relegated to Eastern religions and New Age ideas. Nowadays, however, researchers and the general population are both finding more and more that mindfulness has incredible benefits at helping people deal with the stress and anxiety of daily life. It can actually even help to rewire your brain to be more calm and optimistic!

This book is specifically about mindfulness as a way of helping people who suffer from OCD. Because for many people, OCD is associated with stress and anxiety, and mindfulness can help alleviate some of the symptoms. This book will give you 10 different tips at becoming mindful, as well as some practical steps that you can take towards implementing those tips in your daily life. The intended result is that you will be able to gain more control over your symptoms of OCD and be empowered to live a more productive, fulfilling life.

1 WHAT IS OCD?

Obsessive-Compulsive Disorder, commonly known as OCD, is a mental disorder in which someone feels constant urges to clean something, repeat certain routines or rituals, or have repetitive thought patterns. The person may wash his or her hands repetitively, constantly check the oven knobs to make sure that they are off, constantly check the doors to make sure that they are locked, or constantly count things. For many who suffer from OCD, it has interfered with their daily lives because dealing with the compulsions takes up an hour or more of their time every day, and the repetitive thoughts associated with the disorder keep them from experiencing meaningful relationships and fully engaging in their activities of daily living. In extreme cases, the symptoms can be so damaging that the person is led to contemplate or even attempt suicide.

While the cause of the disorder is unknown, for many people, it is associated with anxiety and stress. A large number of people who have it have experienced a major traumatic event, particularly child abuse but also events such as the death of a loved one or a major car accident. Other causes may include infection and genetics. Half of all cases of OCD present before the age of 20 and development of symptoms after the age of 35 is extremely rare. Worldwide, about 1% of the population is believed to be affected with OCD every year, and approximately 2-3% of the population is affected at some point in their lifetimes.

Treatments for OCD include medication, such as selective serotonin reuptake inhibitors, as well as Cognitive Behavioral Therapy (CBT) to help people learn to deal with the intrusive, repetitive thoughts. One particularly successful method of treating OCD is learning mindfulness. Mindfulness is the practice of being fully aware of what is going on both around and inside of you so that you can distinguish your own negative thoughts from what is actually happening, separate your own feelings from the facts, and not feel the need to treat every thought you have as if you are actually facing a threat.

2 DEEP BREATHING

One of the most beneficial yet most overlooked methods of practicing mindfulness is to engage in deep breathing exercises. You don't have to sit in a lotus position humming "ohm," but if you feel so compelled, then do so. All that you need to do is sit up straight (make sure that your back is as straight as possible), breathe in, and breathe out. Take 10 seconds to inhale and 20 seconds to exhale. Practice this simple exercise for two minutes a day.

The benefits of engaging in deep breathing are so immense that one must wonder why this simple exercise is so often overlooked. One reason why is that it naturally triggers the parasympathetic nervous system, which promotes a relaxation response. It actually causes your body to physiologically relax! Many diseases, including OCD, are either directly or indirectly correlated with stress, and most of us lead busy and stressful lives. Deep breathing is a way to make you consciously slow down and take notice of what is going on inside of you. By being aware of what you are thinking and feeling, you can get a better grasp of what are your own thoughts, which may be distortions of reality, and what is actually going on around you.

One reason why your body starts to feel tense whenever you feel anxious is because you are not breathing deeply. When you breathe shallowly, your body does not receive the oxygen that it needs and is therefore unable to properly fuel your cells. Breathing deeply gets all of the oxygen your body needs to every part of it, enabling your contracted muscles to relax. This response is crucial to helping you get control over the symptoms of OCD. You cannot simply think your way out of OCD; if you could, you probably would have found much relief from your symptoms by now. Your body needs to be in tune with your thoughts; if your body is out of sync because it does not have proper oxygen, you will be unable to control the impulses of OCD. However, having an adequate supply of oxygen will enable your relaxed mind to ward off some of the impulses.

Breathing deeply can even detoxify your body. One of the primary toxins in your body is carbon dioxide; if your lungs are compromised by shallow breathing, you will not be able to expel it correctly and it will build up. Getting rid of toxins like carbon dioxide will allow your mind and body to function better.

Another benefit of deep breathing is that it can even relieve pain and increase happiness. This is because it stimulates the release of hormones such as serotonin, the "happiness hormone." Serotonin naturally alleviates stress and anxiety, so stimulating its release is an ideal way to help you control your OCD.

So take two minutes now and breathe in deeply for 10 seconds. Then exhale for 20 seconds. Do it again a few times. You will notice that you start to feel calm and relaxed after just a couple of minutes.

3 TAKE NOTICE OF YOUR SURROUNDINGS

Many of us have busy lives that we do not take the time to stop and smell the roses and we don't even notice that there are roses! If we do, we don't think about whether they are red, yellow, or pink, or about how pretty they are. We simply are not aware of what is going on around us. One way to practice mindfulness is to stop and take notice of your surroundings.

Look around you for a minute. How many colors do you see? Do you see the color brown? In how many places do you see brown? What about red? Pink? Blue? What is your favorite color? How many times do you see it? Notice how you just slowed your brain down so that it is no longer racing. Do you feel less anxious yet, at least a little bit?

Breathe in deeply through your nose. What do you smell? Coffee? Your coworker's perfume? Something cooking? Does it smell pleasant? Does the smell make you happy or bring to mind any memories? Stop and think about the smells around you. Experience them. Breathe in and out deeply. Are you feeling calmer? Good.

How much time do you spend eating your food? If you are like most people in the modern world, you probably don't spend much time eating. After all, you have to get back to work. There are so many things that you need to do in just a small amount of time! Stop. That kind of thinking provokes anxiety and will trigger OCD symptoms. Try to spend more time eating. Take time to notice what you are eating. How does your food smell? What does it look like? Take each bite slowly. What does it taste like? What is its texture? How do the different textures that you are eating interact with each other? Do you like the textures? Take a sip of something after every three bites. Enjoy your food and fully experience it.

What is that that you hear? Is it a fly or mosquito buzzing around your head? Is it the overhead light making a crackling sound? Is it a conversation going on in the next cubicle? Is it the sound of rain? Are you listening to music? Take a minute and listen to it. No, really listen to it. Pay attention to it. Be aware of the sounds around you and where they are coming from.

Are you sitting at a desk right now? Maybe you are sitting outside in a chair or are relaxing on the sofa. Take a minute and feel it. Run your hands along your desk. What does it feel like?

You should feel more aware of your surroundings by now. Being aware of your surroundings helps you separate your own intrusive thoughts from what is going.

4 SLOW DOWN

Many people are convinced that they have to fill every minute of every day with some kind of activity. As a result, their brains never slow down and they are never able to enter a state of relaxation. They even have impaired sleep because their brains are always wired. Constantly being on the go can actually trick your brain into believing that there is a threat, and your brain has a built-in defense to threats: the fight-or-flight response. Adrenaline and cortisol get released into your body, fueling even more stress and making you feel that you have to work harder and do more. Being too busy can actually trigger your brain to respond as if you are under a threat. There is actually great value in simply slowing down.

Slowing down means that you don't feel the need to fill up every single minute of every single day with activities. You can simply let yourself be. Sit outside on the grass and enjoy the feeling of it on your feet. Enjoy the way that the sun shines on your skin; fully experience the warmth of it. Go play with your dog. Push a kid on the swing. Do something that you enjoy rather than something that feels productive and busy. Too often, we feel that we have to be busy in order for life to be meaningful. However, that is simply not true. Meaning is found in the moments when we slow down and enjoy our surroundings and the people that we are with.

How many times a day do you check your phone? How many times an hour? How long can you go without checking your email or text messages? This is something to be aware of. Constantly checking your phone distracts you from mindfulness because it wires your brain to believe that if you aren't being productive, you are wasting time. Put your phone away and go for a walk. The world can wait. You need to take care of your own self and your own needs.

What keeps you from slowing down? What makes you

believe that you have to be constantly on the go? Do you ever feel that your mind is racing? Does being busy fuel anxious thoughts?

Now take an hour to just relax and let yourself be. Step away from electronics, including the television, and connect with yourself and your environment. How do you feel? Is your mind slowing down? What is happening to your anxious thoughts?

Try to take an hour every day to slow down and just let yourself be. Don't let yourself become distracted and overwhelmed by everything that you think you need to do. Stop and smell the roses.

5 MEDITATE

You've already looked at the benefits of deep breathing, being aware of your surroundings, and slowing down. Tying all of those things together is the art of meditation. Meditation is when you allow your mind to slow down focus on something. If you have ever been kept awake at night by an anxious thought that keeps turning around in your head and that you can't distance yourself from, then you are actually meditating on that anxious thought. However, that kind of meditation is negative. Positive meditation is when you intentionally focus on good or positive things and don't concern yourself with the negative thoughts that try to invade.

Many religions have their own meditative practices that are designed to enhance the individual's spirituality or connection with his or her own spirit. Kabbalah, the Jewish mystical tradition, has meditative practices designed to lift the individual from his or her own daily struggles and into the cognizance of the Eternal One. Christianity adopted some Kabbalistic practices, which are used by Christians to meditate on the Divine. Islam, especially the Sufi branch, also has meditative practices. Some religions, such as Hinduism, Sikhism, and Jainism, find meditation to be so intrinsic to an individual's spiritual well-being that it is a prescribed part of daily life. If you associate yourself with any religion, a good place to start is to learn about what your religion says about meditation and how you should practice it.

If you are not religious and are not interested in what these different religions say about meditation, you can still learn to meditate. Sit up straight and close your eyes. Keep your posture as perfect as you can so that you can breathe in fully and deeply. Inhale for 10 seconds and exhale for 20 seconds. Continue inhaling and exhaling in this manner while you do one of the following:

1. Tell yourself positive things. You are a good person. You are aware of your surroundings and you are mindful of what is going on inside of you. You can overcome your OCD so that it no longer dominates your life.

2. Focus on something positive. This can be an image of the ocean, a favorite childhood memory, or something entirely innocuous, like a door or window frame.

Remain in this state for as long as you can. If you can only meditate for a couple of minutes at first, that's fine. Keep practicing meditation every day and try to remain a bit longer each time.

At first, you may find that you are distracted by things that need to be done. If you try to meditate first thing in the morning, you may be so distracted by the need to get to work on time that you aren't able to meditate successfully. If that's the case, try to find a time that works for you, when you won't be so distracted.

The point of meditation is to empty your mind of negative thoughts so that it can be filled with positivity. Meditation is actually a powerful tool that can rewire your brain to think more positively.

6 DEVELOP CONCENTRATION

Many of us live lives that are so busy that we don't know the value of concentration; and not only that, we don't even know how to concentrate. When was the last time you were able to work for two hours straight without having to check your phone or email? Your answer to that question should give you an indication of how well you are able to concentrate.

A huge part of the problem is that many people actually see distraction as a good thing. They sit on a park bench and stare at their phones instead of watching the ducks in the pond. Many people can't even get through a meal with their friends and/or family without their phones! Be honest with yourself: How much is your phone keeping you from being able to concentrate on your own life?

Being able to concentrate is actually the cornerstone of mindfulness. If you cannot focus on the task at hand because you are so distracted, then there is very little room for you to be aware of your own thoughts, your feelings, the people around you and your environment.

Here are some tips for helping you to develop your ability to concentrate.

1. Turn off and tune out all distractions. If you are used to listening to music or keeping the television on, turn those things off. Put your cell phone on silent or off and tuck it away. Close out all of your internet tabs except for the one that you are currently using.

2. Practice deep breathing and meditation every day. The powerful effect that these exercises have on your mind can help you train it to tune out distractions and focus on the task at hand.

3. Exercise. Exercise helps stimulate the release of hormones that will help you concentrate. It also burns adrenaline and cortisol out of your system, both of which can be a deterrent to concentration.

4. Only try to do one thing at a time. Our society values multitasking, but multitasking is really a myth. You can't focus on two things at once. What actually happens when you try to multitask is your brain constantly jumps between tasks, causing you to do everything more inefficiently. So think about what is the thing that you need to be working on right now, and just do that one thing. Write down everything else that you need to do so that you don't forget, and get to those things in their proper time.

When you are able to concentrate better, those impulsive thoughts associated with OCD will have less room to invade your mind. You will be more focused on what you are actually doing and less concerned about going to wash your hands or make sure that the door is locked. You will also have the tremendous satisfaction of getting your job done well.

7 BE KIND TO YOURSELF

Many of us lead incredibly busy, hectic lives because we are constantly trying to please others. We work so hard to please the boss. We throw a party to please our friends. We cook dinner to please our families. One effect of anxiety is that you can become so tied up in pleasing other people that you don't recognize or appreciate the need to please yourself. If you do, you may talk yourself out of it by saying that you don't have the time or there are too many other things and people that you need to take care of.

However, there is great value in being kind to yourself. Go to the salon and get a manicure and pedicure. Get your hair done. Cook your favorite dinner. Eat dessert without apologizing. Go to the park. Go to the ball game. Rent the movie that you've been wanting to see. Go out with your friends and do something so fun that it's ridiculous.

When you are kind to yourself, you actually increase your own self-esteem and self-awareness. You become more aware of the things that you like and the things that may irritate you or set you off. You may be able to find the things that trigger your compulsions and cause you to have repetitive, negative thoughts. By engaging in the things that you like, you can rewire your brain to actually be more positive. It will release those positive hormones, like serotonin, and even cleanse itself of toxins.

The corollary of being kind to yourself is allowing other people to be kind to you. Let your friends, family, and coworkers show that they appreciate you. If someone wants to give you a gift, don't feel that you have to give one in reciprocity. Many times, we allow ourselves to feel guilty when someone does something kind. That is a mistake. Think of what motive you had last time you did something kind for someone. Was it to get something in return, or was it because you just wanted to be nice? If a friend wants to be nice and buy you dinner, don't feel that you have to do the same. If you want to, great. But don't feel obligated to.

What is your guilty pleasure? Why does it make you feel guilty? What is something that you would really like to do at the end of the day? What keeps you from doing it? How can you deal with the obstacles and anxieties that keep you from being kind to yourself and doing the things that you enjoy?

Be mindful of the things that you enjoy and how they make you feel. Be mindful of why you do or don't allow yourself to partake of these activities. And most importantly, be kind to yourself.

8 JOURNALING

Journaling is a great way to become aware of your own thoughts and feelings. Knowing yourself — being self-aware by understanding your thoughts, actions, motivations, and feelings — is a powerful key to being mindful. Journaling is a great way to help you become more self-aware.

One important aspect of mindfulness in regards to OCD is being able to understand what your triggers are. In other words, what are some things that cause you to have compulsive thoughts? Maybe something that is seemingly innocuous, like a clock or a set of keys, is connected with a particularly stressful or traumatic memory. You may not realize that those things are actually triggers.

Journaling can help you identify your triggers. If you notice yourself having a lot of compulsive thoughts that you just can't seem to get rid of, take out your journal and start writing about what is going on. What exactly is going on around you? What are you thinking? What are you feeling? Who is involved in the situation? What are those people saying or doing? After a while, you may notice a pattern in what you are writing. You may see that certain things are making you particularly nervous or anxious and setting off compulsive thoughts.

Journaling can also help you put some of your nervousness and anxiety to rest. Instead of tossing the same idea around your head for hours and hours, keeping yourself awake at night, write it down. Write down everything that is causing you stress, how that stress feels, and how it impacts your life. You may feel a tremendous sense of release just by writing these things down. Writing out your thoughts has actually been shown to have a healing effect on the mind and body.

There are other ways that journaling can help bring you into a state of mindfulness. It brings you from being annoyed or distracted by your surroundings to helping you become in touch with your own thoughts and feelings about what is going on. It can help in making you aware of your own likes, dislikes, and what you ultimately want out of life.

Here are some ideas that you can journal about.

1. What is something that happened today that made me happy?
2. What is something that happened today that made me feel an unpleasant emotion (pain, anger, sadness, anxiety, etc.)?
3. What compulsive thoughts did I have today? What did I do with those compulsive thoughts? What was the result?
4. What is something that no one else knows about me?

While you can certainly use your computer to journal, there is actually a therapeutic benefit that comes from writing things out on paper. Go on, try it. Get a notebook and pen and start writing. You may find that your mind is instantly set at ease.

9 COUNSELING

There are some counseling methods that have been developed specifically for people who suffer from OCD. One of them is Cognitive Behavioral Therapy (CBT) which teaches people to be aware of their own thought patterns so that they can change them. It is a very effective way for people to develop mindfulness, particularly for people with anxiety and OCD.

The model that CBT uses is that our actions are motivated by our thoughts, which are heavily influenced by our core beliefs. Our core beliefs are basically what we believe about ourselves and the world around us. If our core beliefs say that we are good, valuable, strong, worthy, we can do great things, and our lives matter, then the thoughts that we have will generally be positive and pleasant. We will be able to feel good about ourselves and in return, we can be good to other people. If our core beliefs say that we are insignificant, incapable, unworthy, and life is unfair and that the world is a harsh and demanding place, then negative, anxious thoughts will follow. Those thoughts could be why you have the compulsions that you have.

CBT helps you become aware of the negative thoughts that you have, as well as the core beliefs that shape them so that you can work to change them. Changing negative thoughts to positive ones can have a significant impact on decreasing anxiety and stress and helping you live a happy, meaningful, and purposeful life. By decreasing the stress, you may be able to simultaneously decrease the compulsive thoughts that have been plaguing you. CBT has actually been shown to reduce compulsions by up to 70%. Imagine how much of your life you could get back if you had 70% fewer compulsions.

CBT is not the only type of counseling that can help people with OCD. There is also DBT, or Dialectical Behavioral

Therapy, which functions under a model very similar to the CBT model. In addition to helping you change your core beliefs, DBT helps you gain tools to deal with some of the difficulties that you may face, especially your triggers.

Going to a counselor can be scary and intimidating. If you are worried about what others will think, remember that you are under no obligation to let anybody know. The thought of opening up to somebody that you don't know about all of your fears and anxieties can itself be very anxious. Keep in mind that counselors trained in conducting CBT, DBT, and other forms of therapy. They go through a rigorous process to become licensed. They also receive ongoing training so that they can be aware of the newest research and approaches.

Some counselors have different specialties, such as grief counseling or anger management. Look for a therapist who is specially trained in treating OCD. He or she will probably have both training and experience in helping people like you find freedom from their compulsions.

10 DON'T BE JUDGMENTAL

If you suffer from OCD, the odds are that you are blaming yourself for something that might happen in the future. You probably judge yourself. Very harshly. A lot. However, part of being mindful is accepting your present reality without being judgmental, either of yourself, others, or of the things that are happening. This means that whatever happens, you aren't blaming yourself or the people around you. Yes, maybe you could have done things differently and seen different results. However, you need to recognize that you are not the problem.

Forgive yourself. You are not perfect, and that's OK. You have probably made some mistakes, some of them pretty big. You have probably hurt other people and also hurt yourself. Guess what? So has everyone else on the planet. Instead of being harsh and judgmental on yourself, you need to forgive yourself for not being perfect. This means that you accept yourself just the way you are, your OCD, and all. While you certainly want to minimize the mistakes that you make, you need to recognize that everyone makes mistakes. While some mistakes really aren't OK, and maybe you have made some that aren't OK, you are OK just the way you are. You don't need to change. Love yourself just the way you are.

Forgive others. This one is easier said than done because if you are like anyone else on the planet, you have probably been hurt extensively by the people around you. You may feel that you can never trust another person again. Something that someone else did to you may actually be the reason you have anxiety and OCD. However, forgiveness is the only way to find freedom from what happened. A wise person said that forgiveness is setting a prisoner free and then finding that the prisoner was you.

Forgiving someone doesn't mean that you minimize or forget what that person did. It means that you stare hard at the reality of what happened, acknowledging it fully, and then break ties with it. The process is not simple. It's actually a very, very hard thing to do. You may not be ready to forgive, but maybe you are ready to be ready to forgive. Freeing yourself from all the grudges you have towards your enemy, your life, and even to yourself will give you a long lasting peace. A religious clergy person, therapist, or trusted friend can help you through the process of forgiving those who have hurt you.

Separate yourself from your OCD. You are not your OCD. It is something that you have to contend with. You have to learn how to cope with it, and you are learning to cope with it because you have read this far in this book. However, it does not define you. It does not make you the wonderful person that you are.

10 LET GO AND HAVE FUN

While for some people having fun is the air that they breathe, for many people with OCD, it can actually be quite a challenge. After all, how are you supposed to stop worrying about the oven knobs or front door? What should you do when the anxious, repetitive thoughts arise? What if people find out that you're crazy?

Relax. You aren't crazy. However, if you have been suffering from OCD for a while, your brain is probably wired in such a way that having fun may actually be a challenge. Loosening up is hard to do when you have intense anxiety and are constantly worrying.

However, getting out and having fun can be a powerful tool in dealing with your anxiety. Maybe you feel like you are not allowed to have fun, or that you are doomed to be miserable. And who are you to mess with fate? Sometimes, just getting out of the house is an achievement. While it will probably be hard at first, your brain will release the hormones that will naturally cause you to be happy and banish some of your anxiety.

If you find that you are too anxious to leave the house, consider having someone come over for a visit. You can have dinner together and then watch a movie. You may worry about whether or not the other person will actually have fun. If that's the case, let the other person pick out what movie to watch and/or what to eat. Be kind to yourself and don't try to do more than you are able.

Before you go out or have someone come over, you may need to prepare yourself by practicing some mindfulness. Start by doing some deep-breathing exercises. Meditate to help you banish your anxious thoughts and replace them with positive ones. After all, you really are going to have a good time and enjoy yourself! Are you feeling stressed about going out? Write in your journal about how you feel. What about going out makes you feel stressed? Why do you think you have that trigger? What can you do to help release the anxiety so that you can enjoy yourself as much as possible?

For those who are intentionally self-aware, going out and having fun can actually be the epitome of mindfulness. You intentionally experience things that you enjoy and give you pleasure. You relish the experience of pleasure by appreciating every moment, all of the people that you are with, what you are doing, and the opportunity to have fun. If you have OCD and are working on being mindful, you can intentionally create memories that you can look back on and relive in your mind when you are feeling particularly stressed or anxious.

CONCLUSION

Mindfulness is for everyone. It enables us to slow down and actually experience our lives rather than racing through them at breakneck speed. It keeps us from judging ourselves and the people around us and helps us to accept things as they are. You probably know plenty of people who can benefit from that kind of outlook.

For people with OCD, there are particular benefits to mindfulness that can actually decrease the symptoms and compulsions and help them live a more meaningful, satisfying life. If you have OCD, you can follow the above guidelines for mindfulness to help you decrease your anxiety and find relief from your compulsions. Mindfulness seems like a rather easy thing.

So easy that one might think it is mindless! However, nothing could be further from the truth. Disciplining yourself to do deep-breathing is hard. Meditating is hard. It means deliberately focusing your attention away from the negative thoughts that probably fill your mind nearly every minute of every day. Journaling is relaxing and healing, but no one said that it is easy. Slowing down your busy life, especially when you have filled it with busyness to avoid your pain and anxiety, is hard.

Turning off your cell phone is hard. And forgiving people who have hurt you, truly facing the pain that you have experienced and relinquishing your right to judge the person who inflicted it on you, there is nothing easy about that. These are all habits that you have to intentionally form. They don't just happen.

You may need to find a professional therapist to help guide you through the process of becoming mindful and thereby decreasing your symptoms of OCD. You will probably also want to find people, such as friends and family, who can support you. Maybe they will want to join in on your journey to mindfulness and you can hold each other accountable for practicing mindfulness techniques every day. The journey will be hard. However, the end results will be well worth the effort. You will find freedom from many of your compulsions and be able to get your life back.

CW01314023

IN GOD WE TRUST

IN GOD WE TRUST

(Not in Lying Liberal Lunatics)

JOE HOFT

Copyright © 2020 Joe Hoft

All rights reserved.

ISBN-13: 9798611062340

DEDICATION

This book is dedicated to the people who demand and fight for truth and justice everywhere, for we know where happiness lies. Together we can save the world

CONTENTS

Acknowledgments · ix

1 Introduction ·1
   The Status of the US in 2015 After Seven Years of President Obama · · ·1
   The Status of the US after Three Years of President Trump · · · · · · · · ·6
      The Stock Markets ·6
      US Debt to GDP ·8
      Food Stamps ·9
      China Is No Longer Close to the US in GDP · · · · · · · · · · · · ·9
      Annual Report of Economic Freedom of the World · · · · · · · · · ·13
      Companies Coming Back to the US · · · · · · · · · · · · · · · · · ·13
      Public Confidence ·15
2 Truth and Honesty from our Media ·17
   The Demise of the Fourth Estate – The Media · · · · · · · · · · · · · · ·17
      Truth in the Media Crumbles Communism · · · · · · · · · · · · · ·18
      The Media Distorts the Truth ·20
      The Media Creates Conspiracies · · · · · · · · · · · · · · · · · · ·21
      The Media Uses Polls to Manipulate · · · · · · · · · · · · · · · · ·22
      The Media Reports Only One Side of an Issue · · · · · · · · · · · ·26
      The Media Reports Outright Lies · · · · · · · · · · · · · · · · · · ·28
      The Media Doesn't Report Stories It Doesn't Like · · · · · · · · · ·29
      The Media's Links to Liberalism · · · · · · · · · · · · · · · · · · ·33
   The Trump Years – 'Fake News' Becomes 'Corrupt' · · · · · · · · · · · ·35
   New Media is the Answer ·39

Controlling Internet and Social Media · · · · · · · · · · · · · · · · · · · 41

Stopping Social Media's Attacks Against Conservatives · · · · · · · · 44

A Case Study: The Gateway Pundit · 50

3 Truth and Honesty from our Politicians · · · · · · · · · · · · · · · · · · 56

Politicians Are Above the Law · 58

Politicians and Money · 61

The Schiff Show · 65

Congressional and Supreme Court Record Holders · · · · · · · · · · 72

(At the very least) Institute Term Limits · · · · · · · · · · · · · · · 74

4 Truth and Honesty from our Government · · · · · · · · · · · · · · · · · 76

The Federal Reserve (The FED) · 76

The Corrupt Deep State · 83

Obama's Habitual Spying · 84

The Lead Up to the Mueller Hoax · · · · · · · · · · · · · · · · · · · 92

Crowdstrike's Confirmation · 98

Mueller's Next Steps · 105

Concord Management's Grapes of Wrath · · · · · · · · · · · · · · 111

5 Conclusion · 117

Appendix I · 125

Jim Hoft Statement for the Subcommittee on the
Constitution and Civil Justice · 125

Bibliography · 129

Index · 151

About The Author · 155

Acknowledgments

Many thanks to those who demand the truth today. It is not easy finding the truth with the media and now the social media in cahoots with lying liberal lunatic politicians and government bureaucrats. Americans and truth seekers around the world must work to find the truth. Please never give up. Demand the truth and continue to fight for it. The truth can't be broken, and it will ultimately help us in our journey in this life. Our biggest challenges remain within ourselves. We must demand a world where we can seek and discover the beauty that we possess. This can only take place in an environment of freedom, with protections for everyone's individual rights.

1

INTRODUCTION

*I*N *2014, DONALD Trump was known as the celebrity billionaire on the TV show 'The Apprentice'. There was no indication at that time that Mr. Trump would soon be running for President of the United States in the most talked about election in US history. There was certainly no hint that he would become the 45th President of the US. Now after three years of his Presidency we know that there are some individuals we can trust and some lying lunatics that we can't.*

THE STATUS OF THE US IN 2015 AFTER SEVEN YEARS OF PRESIDENT OBAMA

In early 2015, Ronald Reagan's first director of the Office of Management and Budget, David Stockman, noted specific concerns with the rising stock market which he claimed were propped up by the actions of the Federal Reserve. He stated that the problem with the 'Fed' is that they think that interest rates are some magic elixir that will cause the very troubled and difficult economy to revive. Because of this, Stockman believed that **stocks were set to plunge**.[1]

In an interview with the BBC in February 2015, Alan Greenspan, the former Chief of the US Federal Reserve for over 18 years serving under Presidents

---

1 (Rosenberg, 2015)

Reagan, Bush Sr., Clinton and Bush Jr.,[2] made the following statements after discussing the budget challenges in the US:

> "…there's another problem here which is basically that the **debt has now gotten to a point in the United States as a percent of GDP** that's crowding out a goodly part of capital investment. It's not a large issue but it's a growing issue and unless we come to grips with this problem, we're going to have a problem which could be very well the size of the problem that the Euro is. We're in a position where we've got fundamental fiscal problems in this country which politically we don't want to address. Neither party wants to address them. I'm afraid we're going to run into some form of political crisis…"[3]

On top of all the fiscal challenges related to the debt and deficits from the dysfunctional social programs in America, the quantitative easing (QE) economy and its global effects were reaching a pinnacle. The economic prophet who foresaw the Lehman crisis with uncanny accuracy, William White, from Switzerland, was even more worried about the world's financial system going into 2015 than he was in 2008. All the world's major central banks are encouraging asset bubbles deliberately to put off the day of reckoning. White called the world "dangerously unanchored," with "no idea where this is going to end."[4]

In addition to the Fed manipulating interest rates, other contributors to the fiscal challenges facing the US were the archaic and dysfunctional social programs and the nearly one third of Americans receiving some sort of welfare benefit. Census data released in 2014 revealed that nearly 110 million Americans – more than one-third of the country – were receiving government assistance of some kind. This number counted people receiving federal benefits, or subsidies based on income, including welfare programs ranging from food stamps to subsidized housing to the program where the government provides cash to

---

2 (Harress, 2013)

3 (Mardell, 2015; Mardell, 2015)

4 (Evens-Pritchard, 2015)

IN GOD WE TRUST

those in need called, "Temporary Assistance for Needy Families". According to the Census Bureau, at the end of 2012, **51.5 million were on food stamps**, while 83 million were collecting Medicaid – with some benefitting from multiple programs.[5]

The US's social programs were created to help those in need, but some analysts worried that the way they were designed increasingly incentivized people not to work. When recipients combine several government assistance programs, in many cases, they are paid better to stay at home than to go to work. The Cato Institute's Michael Tanner said that in eight of the most generous states, the benefits can be tantamount to a $20 minimum wage – which would exceed the $7.25 minimum wage in place in most states. According to Tanner, "You can't in the long run have a society in which you have to rely on a smaller and smaller group of wealth producers who have to support more and more people who are not contributing to that wealth."[6]

Despite all the efforts to help the poor in America, the number of poor people was increasing. In October 2014 the US Census Bureau reported that more than 48 million Americans were living in poverty.[7] The Stanford Center on Poverty and Income Inequality noted in its 2014 Annual Report that "the country's economy and labor market remain in deep disrepair".[8] To anyone in the US today without a job, there were government programs that would help, but in 2015 without new jobs, the situation was desperate.

The drag on the economy of these social programs which also burden the working class was becoming more apparent. In late 2014 the IMF noted that **China had taken over the US as the world's largest economy**. According to the IMF, China had an economy of $17.6 trillion in GDP while the US had an economy of $17.4 trillion. Although the IMF's measurements may not agree with other projections, this was the first time that the US was not rated with the number one economy in the world in decades.[9]

---

5 (Emanuel, 2014)

6 Ibid

7 (Gillespie, 2014)

8 (Grusky, 2014)

9 (Foxnews.com, 2014)

The implications of the fiscal freefall in the US were in action. The 2014 *Annual Report of Economic Freedom of the World* **found that the US ranked 12th among 152 countries**, tied with the United Kingdom, and lower than neighbor Canada or Australia. The Annual Report is published by the Cato Institute and Canada's Fraser Institute and has been published since 1996. In 2000 the US ranked 2nd in the world in terms of boasting a free economy. The actions that led to the US's declining ranking were expected to lower future economic growth.[10]

The Freedom Index was built on decades of research by Nobel laureates and dozens of leading scholars. It measures five categories that impact the economy: 1. Size of government; 2. Legal structure and security of property rights; 3. Access to sound money; 4. Freedom to trade internationally; and, 5. Regulation of Credit, Labor and Business. Countries where citizens are freer to engage in business and trade and countries where property and legal rights are protected by the rule of law will score higher on the index. According to economic research, the countries that rate higher in the survey will also do better economically and create and generate more wealth. The five freest economies in the world are: Hong Kong, Singapore, New Zealand, Switzerland and Mauritius.[11]

The chief factor behind the US decline in the Freedom Index was related to the country's legal structure. The report noted that the rule of law has long been the foundation of America's economic prosperity and liberty but the US ranking in this area had plummeted to a terrible 36th place in the world. The report observed that to a large degree, the US had experienced a significant move away from rule of law and toward a highly regulated, politicized, and heavily policed state.[12]

Some **forward looking companies were seeing the signs and moved their corporate headquarters outside of the US**. In August of 2014 the fast food chain Burger King announced that it would spend some $11

---

10 (Flynn, 2014)

11 Ibid

12 Ibid

IN GOD WE TRUST

billion to buy Tim Hortons Inc., a Canadian breakfast food chain, and then merge Burger King into it, thereby turning what was once a major American company into a major Canadian company. The reason behind this action was to move the company's headquarters to Canada, where corporate taxes were significantly lower.[13]

This process of companies moving to other countries is called inversion and it occurred more and more often, despite the fascistic suggestion by the Obama administration that headquartering outside the United States represented a betrayal of God and country. One expert reported, "Overall, some 25 major companies have participated in tax inversions since President Obama took office. That trend will continue to accelerate as President Obama ratchets up the rhetoric and threatens harsher action against companies that dare to buck his high-tax priorities."[14]

Not only were companies recognizing the challenges facing the situation in the US, individuals were too. A New York Times poll in 2014 showed that **the public was more pessimistic than it was after the 2008 financial crisis in the idea that it is possible to work hard and become rich**. Only 64% of Americans' polled on a wide range of economic and financial issues, said they still believed in the American dream, the lowest result in roughly two decades. In early 2009, near the depth of the financial crisis, 72% of Americans still believed that hard work could result in riches.[15]

The US was becoming what Ayn Rand in the book *Atlas Shrugged* prophesized so many years ago. Working Americans were being asked to support more and more. In the Obama years the average working American was forgotten.

Clearly, some things were wrong with the US in 2015, towards the end of Obama's Presidency. The country was financially bankrupt, and people were seeing it. Americans wanted real change.

The trust in politicians and the media was at all-time lows, as the truth seemed to be something of a luxury, rather than a mandate from

---

13 (Shapiro, 2014)

14 Ibid

15 (Thee-Brenan, 2014)

— 5 —

the people. Government policies led to the feeling of insecurity in the US and thousands of deaths abroad. Actions were necessary to preserve the future of this great country and the world.

THE STATUS OF THE US AFTER THREE YEARS OF PRESIDENT TRUMP

President Trump won the Republican primaries and then the Presidency over Democrat Hillary Clinton in November 2016. Immediately things changed, and in some cases, even before his inauguration.

THE STOCK MARKETS

Members of the media like Paul Krugman from the New York Times shrieked that the markets would collapse, and the US would be led by people that didn't understand economics like he did. They were doomed to fail. Krugman claimed that the world would fall into a global recession because of the results of Donald Trump winning the 2016 Presidential election.[16]

Fortunately for the US and the world, Krugman couldn't be more wrong. The markets roared after President Trump won the election and three years later they haven't stopped (with the exception of the crazy Fed increasing rates to the point of almost setting the US into a recession in late 2018).

The following information was from a post that I posted at The Gateway Pundit in November 2019. Note that the Mainstream Media (MSM) hasn't taken the time to calculate or report any of this. If it's good news related to President Trump, it is left to a Trump supporter in Hong Kong to get this out.

At of the end of November 2019, the stock markets were in the middle of their greatest stock market rally ever. The DOW reached its 118th all-time high since the 2016 election and 101st since President Trump's inauguration.

---

16 (Krugman, 2016)

IN GOD WE TRUST

After President Trump was elected the stock markets exploded. The markets are a gauge of the economy and include expectations of the future. On November 8th, 2016, the DOW stood at 18,333. Since that date, and after Donald Trump won the 2016 election, the DOW has soared. Yesterday [November 26, 2019] the DOW closed at another new all-time high of 28,122 – 9,789 points higher than the day of the 2016 election!

Never has the DOW risen so much in such a short period of time. THIS IS HISTORIC! Not only has the DOW skyrocketed since Donald Trump was elected President, the market's rise is record breaking.

President Trump's first year in office (2017) saw the most all-time stock market closing highs (71) as well as the largest single year increase in DOW history (4,956 points). Prior to 2017, no year in the DOW's more than 100-year history ever saw the DOW increase by more than 3,500 points, let alone 4,900. The most all-time highs in a year prior to 2017 was 69 in 1995.

Since President Trump was elected President the DOW tied the record for the most all-time closing highs in a row. In January of 1987 President Reagan saw the DOW increase to new all-time highs a record 12 days in a row. In February of 2017, President Trump matched Reagan's record.

The DOW reached its fastest 500-point increase between major milestones under President Trump. In January of 2018 the DOW surpassed 26,000 and six days later the DOW surpassed 26,500. Under President Trump the DOW has seen the fastest 1,000; 2,000; 3,000; 4,000; 5,000; 6,000; 7,000, 8,000 and 9,000 point increases in DOW history. No similar records occurred at any time in history.

Also, President Trump didn't ride an Obama wave, the DOW under Obama was down in 2015 and stayed relatively flat until the 2016 election. The DOW is now officially up more than 50% since the 2016 election.

Presidents GW Bush and Obama NEVER reached a new all-time high in their entire first terms. Presidents (Franklin) Roosevelt,

Truman and Carter never reached a new all-time high in their Presidencies.

President Trump has now increased the markets by more than any other President in their entire Presidency (when counting from their election win to the election day in their last year in office.) As noted above, under President Trump the DOW has increased 9,789 over the past three years. This has never happened before.[17]

US DEBT TO GDP

President Obama raised the amount of debt and the amount of 'debt to GDP' astronomically. When Obama took over in 2009, the amount of US debt was around $10 trillion but by the end of 2016, eight years later, the debt had doubled to nearly $20 trillion.

The following information is from a post of mine published at the Gateway Pundit in October 2019.

Obama also increased the US debt to GDP ratio. In 2009, when Obama took over, the US debt to GDP ratio was around 68%. By the end of Obama's terms in 2016, the ratio had climbed to 105%. This too was moving in the right direction under President Trump after three years.

...when comparing the amount of US Debt from the government's daily report of debt to the amount of GDP from the current GDP release, the amount of debt to GDP is decreasing under President Trump (a very good thing).

The ratio of debt to GDP is decreasing drastically – from 105.3% when Obama was President to 103.2% at the end of the 2nd Quarter of 2019! (Note that Obama increased the Debt to GDP ratio by 30% over his first two years and more than 40% during his two terms in

---

17 (Hoft J. , Want Evidence the Fed Stalled the Trump Rally? 11 of Past 19 Days Since the Fed Lowered the Fed Funds Rate the DOW Hit All-Time Highs, 2019)

IN GOD WE TRUST

office. Also, under Obama the Fed kept rates at 0% for his first seven years!)

If President Trump had the same luxury of a 0% interest rate as Obama the Debt to GDP would be much less because US debt would be $1 trillion less.

More than one trillion of the two trillion increase in debt under President Trump is due to the Fed's increase in rates.[18]

FOOD STAMPS

As noted above, at the end of 2012, there were 51.5 million Americans on food stamps. This is one measure of the number of individuals in poverty. Obama's solution to helping the poor was to give them government handouts.

President Trump's answer to reducing the number of individuals and families in poverty is to get them jobs. This strategy is working. By September of 2019 the number of individuals on food stamps had decreased by 6.2 million individuals and 2.9 million households since the beginning of President Trump's administration.[19]

The policy of reducing unemployment and providing jobs to individuals not only reduces government costs but it also has a spiritual aspect. When individuals are unemployed and not able to earn a living, they become very depressed. This is one reason why so many people on welfare begin dabbling in drugs and crime. Idle hands are the devil's work shop, and this is obvious when looking into the communities with high unemployment and poverty. The loving answer is to provide these individuals jobs. This is what President Trump has done.

CHINA IS NO LONGER CLOSE TO THE US IN GDP

When President Trump took over the US in January 2017, he inherited a mess. Perhaps nothing was as messed up as US relations with China. The Obama team had succumbed to every move and request from the China regime and Obama's

---

18 (Hoft J. , Winning, Winning, Winning! President Trump Decreases Debt to GDP Ratio Indicating Economy Growing Faster than US Debt!, 2019)
19 (Rodriguez, 2019)

— 9 —

Vice President Biden was involved in a billion dollar transaction between the Chinese and his son.

President Trump addressed this quickly and directly. He first and immediately met with the Chinese leader Xi Jinping. Then after building a relationship with Xi, President Trump began to address the issues.

In just two short years, the dynamic between the US and China changed. At the end of 2018, the US economy surged to a GDP amount of over $20.5 trillion.[20] The US economy was on fire. The opposite was true of China. It's GDP at the end of 2018 was reported by the World Bank at $13.6 trillion.[21] China was no longer the top economy in the world by far. As a matter of fact, it was only a portion (two third's) of the US's economy.

The following information is from a post of mine published at The Gateway Pundit in August 2019. Living in Hong Kong, I have made numerous trips in and out of China which provide me with a perception that few people have.

The Chinese were relentless in their efforts to obtain Western technology and grow their economy. They set up trade barriers and manipulated their currency in ways that helped China. The US was at a disadvantage in trade resulting in massive deficits in the billions.[22]

Along comes the Trump Administration, the first administration to address China's unfair trade advantage. The timing of Trump's tariffs is not good for China as there are more pressing issues that must be addressed. President Trump is a shrewd negotiator and he obviously believes now is the time to encourage China to make changes to their trade barriers with the US. China may have no choice but to go with what the US offers to keep its economy afloat.[23]

---

20 (Bank, US GDP, 2019)

21 (Bank, China GDP, 2019)

22 (Hoft J. , MUST READ... TRUMP IS RIGHT! China Is In Terrible Economic Condition; Cannot Afford to Lose the US Market, 2019)

23 Ibid

IN GOD WE TRUST

The more pressing issues for China surround real estate, in a manner similar to the US in 2008. As China grew, it invested in its infrastructure and in addition, it invested in large housing projects throughout the country. These efforts helped bolster China's already fast-growing economy.[24]

The problem is that China over invested in these random properties all over China and these properties today remain empty.[25]

There simply are not enough people in the area where these massive complexes were built that make enough money to afford living in these communities. It appears that the Chinese communists misunderstanding of supply and demand economics may be their downfall.

Some say, no problem, China will just move all the peasants to these massive complexes. This will be devastating. First of all, China needs to feed them. Secondly, as we have learned in the US, people on the dole with no work tend to get involved in drugs and crime. The human spirit needs a purpose – idle hands are the devil's workshop![26]

These many properties throughout China sit unoccupied, and there is a cost to this. Bloomberg reported in September 2018:

Cash-to-short-term debt levels at more than 80 publicly traded real estate companies tracked by Bloomberg were 133 percent on average in the first half, the worst since the first six months of 2015 and down from 297 percent a year earlier. Almost a quarter of developers sport a ratio below 50 percent.[27]

In addition, Bloomberg noted -

But while business has been booming, developers have also been piling on the debt. Firms have been selling more bonds in the domestic market — and at the cheapest rates as investors shrug off default concerns. Those with dollar-denominated obligations, meanwhile, face

---

24 Ibid

25 Ibid

26 Ibid

27 (Bloomberg, 2018)

higher borrowing costs as the U.S. Federal Reserve continues on its tightening path.[28]

The amount of debt related to China's over development is massive. The total amount is unknown with S&P estimating the amount not reported by local communities and banks being over $6 trillion:

China may be sitting on a hidden debt pile of as much as 40 trillion yuan ($6 trillion), concealed off-balance-sheet by the country's local governments, according to research from S&P Global Ratings.[29]

Many local governments in China raise debt and hold it off their balance sheet, in order to avoid lending limits imposed by central authorities. S&P says that this is a growing problem within the country, and that the amount of debt held this way has likely ballooned in recent years.[30]

The government may have to take over these debts as they become insolvent –

Not only is the level of hidden debt held by local governments in the world's second largest economy rising, but so too is the risk of those debts being defaulted on. Much of the debt is held by so-called local government financing vehicles (LGFVs), and S&P reports that central government may be willing to let these vehicles file for bankruptcy in the future.[31]

"Default risk of LGFVs is on the rise. China has opened up the possibility of insolvent LGFVs filing for bankruptcy, but managing the default aftermath is a formidable task for top leadership," the report noted....[32]

The country's total non-financial sector debt, which includes household, corporate and government debt, will surge to almost 300%

---

28 Ibid

29 (Martin, 2018)

30 Ibid

31 Ibid

32 Ibid

of GDP by 2022, up from 242% in 2016. Fears abound that if this debt pile continues to grow, a spectacular blow up could be imminent.[33]

China's financial crash may make the 2008 crash in the US look small. The implications will no doubt impact the entire world. This is why China can't afford to mess around with President Trump and must put together a treaty as soon as possible.[34]

As China falls the US economy will be the one the world runs to and so the impact to the US will be a massive inflow of money resulting in rising markets due to capital infusions.[35]

This is all panning out today. The GDP numbers prove it.

ANNUAL REPORT OF ECONOMIC FREEDOM OF THE WORLD

As noted above in the 2014 *Annual Report of Economic Freedom of the World* the US ranked 12th among 152 countries, tied with the United Kingdom, and lower than neighbor Canada or the land down under, Australia. By 2019, under President Trump the US moved up to fifth place in the entity's Annual Report.[36]

COMPANIES COMING BACK TO THE US

After the 2016 election and even before his inauguration, President-elect Trump was fast working for the American people. One area of focus was on jobs. One by one the President-elect began calling US companies that were working abroad or were in the process of relocating to another country and he encouraged them to stay in the US. The list of companies was large.

A partial list shows that more than one million jobs were saved due to the President-elect's actions before he was even sworn into office:

---

33 Ibid

34 Op cit, Hoft, MUST READ...

35 Ibid

36 (James Gwartney, 2019)

Jobs Created/Saved by Trump

Date	Company	Jobs Added
11/17/2016	Ford	4,700
11/29/2016	Carrier	1,100
12/6/2016	SoftBank	50,000
12/7/2016	Foxconn Technology Group	Unknown
12/13/2016	IBM	25,000
12/29/2016	Sprint	5,000
1/4/2017	Ford	700
1/5/2017	Stanley Black and Decker	1,200
1/9/2017	Fiat	2,000
1/9/2017	Toyota	Unknown
1/10/2017	Alibaba	1,000,000
1/13/2017	Amazon	100,000
1/13/2017	Lockheed Martin	1,800
1/17/2017	General Motors	1,000
1/17/2017	Walmart	34,000
1/17/2017	Hundai/Kia	Unknown
		1,226,500

But this was just the beginning. Once his tax plan was passed in late 2017, the market really took off and American companies then had real incentives to hire and build in America. The job and unemployment numbers as a result were staggering.

After less than three years in office, in November 2019, the results were in. In November alone, the President added another 288,000 new jobs. Unemployment was lowered to a 50 year low of 3.5%. Three years after the 2016 election, President Trump had added 6.8 million jobs. In comparison, President Obama at this same time in office had lost (2.1) million jobs. The difference was nearly 9 million jobs. More Americans were working than any time in US history. The stock markets were at all-time highs and Americans' 401k's had grown more than 50% in less than three years since the 2016 election.[37]

---

37 (Statistics, 2019)

Public Confidence

Despite constant headwinds from Democrats, corrupt members of the 'Deep State' and the ultraliberal and biased media, after only three years of the Trump Presidency, the US was in some ways in its best position ever. The economy was on fire and arguably its best ever. Foreign policy initiatives, such as destroying ISIS in the Middle East and initiating trade deals that helped the US, were in place. The list of President Trump's accomplishments was long and impressive. America was winning again.

Even far-left CNN performed a poll in December 2019 and reported that American's perceptions of the economy were the best in decades:

> Overall, 35 percent of respondents said that economic conditions were "very good," and 41 percent said they were "somewhat good." According to CNN's analysis of the data, the 76 percent net positive is the largest share of Americans to feel good about the economy since 2001, when 80 percent of those queried said things were going well.[38]

Much was accomplished in only three years of the Trump Presidency. The accomplishments were miraculous really. But there is so much is left to do.

The biggest challenge for Americans today revolves around the topic of trust.

Truth and honesty are the foundation for any healthy relationship, whether the relationship be with ourselves, others or our government. When there is no honesty, there is no trust and trust is the building block of all relationships, the cornerstone with which nothing can be built without. Our forefathers wrote in the Declaration of Independence that we were born with inalienable rights, among which the rights to life, liberty and the pursuit of happiness. None of these rights can be in place without trust.

---

38 (Dodge, 2019)

JOE HOFT

Trust is the cornerstone behind the US constitution. It was one thing to produce such a magnificent document but even more important to implement a government system based on the document. Good men led the US in its early years who showed their integrity through their actions and Americans trusted them to do what was right. Today the most essential ingredient lacking in the US is trust. Americans do not trust the media or politicians and this lack of trust may be at all-time highs. As the University of Tennessee law professor Glenn Reynolds wrote in a USA Today in May 2016 – "High-trust societies are much nicer places to live than low-trust ones. But a fish rots from the head and the head of our society is looking pretty rotten."[39]

Lack of trust is one issue, but perhaps more frightening is placing trust in the hands of those who cannot be trusted. When the politicians in the US make a statement or say something that is not true, and it is not pointed out by the media as being untrue, then the result is confusion and the promotion of something not true or even a lie. Any principle built on a lie cannot last like the building with a cornerstone made of sand.

It is the duty of Americans to seek the truth, the duty of politicians to speak the truth, the duty of the government to act honestly and with integrity, and the duty of the media to identify and accurately communicate what is true and what is not.

---

39 (Reynolds, 2016)

2

Truth and Honesty from our Media

WHEN THE MEDIA promotes the truth, evil crumbles and the result is trust. Because of the media's duty to report the truth and uncover lies emanating from the government, the media has often been referred to as the "Fourth Estate". This phrase was first coined by Edmund Burke, an 18th century British political philosopher. He noted that the "three estates" present in the Parliament were the king, the lords, and the commons. But, according to Burke, there was a "Fourth Estate" that trumped them all – the press.[40]

THE DEMISE OF THE FOURTH ESTATE – THE MEDIA

One of the most alarming realities of the current era in the United States and other Western nations is the demise of the Fourth Estate. This destruction occurred when a vigorous and free press became a propaganda organ for the socialist left. As mainstream print and broadcast journalists veered increasingly to the left, the right has responded with its own conservative media

---

40 (Henley, 2012)

JOE HOFT

establishment. The right's move to establish media outlets was a necessary and automatic development, and vital for countering leftist propaganda. However, the demise of the Fourth Estate means there's not much in the middle to probe for the truth buried somewhere beneath the shrills and shills of left and right. There are now few venues that people trust to give them the plain, unspun facts.[41]

Like the good counselor who tries to uncover the facts that the patient is hiding, Americans need to know the facts every politician or administration tries to keep hidden. Americans and the world needed to know the truth about the deaths of four Americans in Benghazi. Americans needed to know the information behind the US going to war in Iraq. Americans needed to know what Bill Clinton and Monica Lewinsky were up to in the Oval Office, as this was pertinent to a criminal case outstanding at the time, and it ultimately impacted Americans' trust in the President. Americans as well needed to know about Watergate and what involvement the President had.[42]

The third US President, Thomas Jefferson said, "If it were left to me to decide whether we should have a government without a free press or a free press without a government, I would prefer the latter". Jefferson knew that our hard-won liberty would be in danger if mostly propaganda organs and agenda-driven tabloids are in place. This would lead to almost no true Fourth Estate.[43]

TRUTH IN THE MEDIA CRUMBLES COMMUNISM
My brother Jim Hoft, the founder and sole proprietor of one of the largest political websites in the US (www.thegatewaypundit.com), first brought this to my attention. When he was in Washington DC receiving an award for his work, he used the following story in his acceptance speech to share why his website was so successful.

'Radio Free Europe' provides an example of how the power of the truth used by the media can materialize into lifesaving blessings for millions. This

---

41 Ibid

42 Ibid

43 Ibid

IN GOD WE TRUST

program was established at the beginning of the Cold War to transmit uncensored news and information to audiences behind the Iron Curtain in communist run Europe. Radio Free Europe broadcast its program inside and outside of the Communist countries. The truth was not being shared with the people under the Communist regimes who were told that everything in their country was great and much better than in the democratically run Western countries of Europe and the US. This was a pile of lies.

Because the Communist leaders did not like the competing true message being shared by Radio Free Europe, the Communists jammed the frequency of its programming and scrambled the message. When this happened, Radio Free Europe would change frequencies until the Communists would eventually catch up and re-scramble the frequency. This process went on and on for several years.[44]

As the iron curtain began to fall, increasing numbers of dissidents and other regime opponents began to challenge the communist system. The leading international broadcaster in many countries behind the Iron Curtain was Radio Free Europe which provided a "megaphone" through which independent figures—denied normal access to local media—could reach millions of their countrymen with uncensored writings. One leader, Nobel laureate Lech Walesa, told an audience in 1989 that the messages from the western press through radios were instrumental in Poland's struggle for freedom and this importance "cannot even be described. Would there be earth without the sun?"[45]

The Radio Free Europe experience shows that as a government leans more towards a dictatorial or communist state, the more energy the government spends on the messages shared by the media. This is the case in Communist China today. China censors the Internet and maintains highly authoritarian policies throughout the country but especially in ethnic minority areas such as Tibet, Xinjiang, and Inner Mongolia. Although China spends much on its defense budget, the government spends more on "social stability maintenance" expenses.[46]

---

44 (RFE/RL, n.d.)

45 Ibid

46 (HRW, 2012)

— 19 —

China's government continues to violate domestic and international legal guarantees of freedom of press and expression by restricting bloggers, journalists, and an estimated more than 500 million Internet users in what they say and write. The government requires Internet search firms and state media to censor issues deemed officially "sensitive". China also blocks access to foreign websites including Facebook, Twitter, and YouTube.[47] This massive effort in China to control the information streaming to its people is exhaustive and expensive.

China's Internet czar, Lu Wei, is the ambassador of an assertive new policy in which China claims the right to block websites, censor content and track users within its borders. In his rise to become China's Internet custodian, he tightened restrictions in what is already the world's most sophisticated system of online censorship. He has curbed the country's social media pioneers by issuing stern warnings in private meetings and restricting the accounts of some. Under his tenure, the government has increased blocks on foreign websites and issued new regulations to restrict sharing on social media and increase censorship of popular online video sites.[48]

A more obscure observation related to Radio Free Europe and China today is that **people want the truth so much that they will work for it**. When the channel for Radio Free Europe was changed, the people behind the iron curtain found the new frequency.

Still today around the world people want the truth and will go many lengths to find it. It really comes down to this – *People who want the truth want freedom of the press but people who want power want control over the press.*

THE MEDIA DISTORTS THE TRUTH

In early 2015 information was uncovered that one of the kings of major media, NBC Nightly News anchor Brian Williams, had lied when referring to an experience of his in Iraq during the Iraq War. Williams stated on the air that he

---

47 Ibid

48 (Perlez, 2014)

IN GOD WE TRUST

was in a helicopter that was hit by an RPG and was forced to land. After being found out, he said that he was in a helicopter behind the one that was hit. It was later found out that he was not following a chopper hit by an RPG but was in a different company altogether. He then was accused of other lies like where he stated that early in the Iraq War he had flown to Iraq with SEAL Team 6 or that he was in Berlin when the wall fell.[49] After some consternation, Williams was put on a temporary leave of absence from the nightly MSM broadcast.

Today there is a lack of trust in the media in the US which leads to controversy and discontent. The Williams case is only one of many reasons why Americans do not trust the media. Often Americans argue over events, proposals, laws and elections because they do not have all the information needed to make a good decision or because they have been given information that is not accurate from the MSM. It would be so refreshing for society if all members were armed with the truth from the media. If we had the truth, decisions would be much easier.

THE MEDIA CREATES CONSPIRACIES

The more the media distorts the truth, the more difficult it is for people to know what the truth is and as a result, conspiracy theories abound. Academic John Naughton, one of three lead investigators in a major Cambridge University project to investigate the impact of conspiracy theories on democracy said that the reason we have conspiracy theories is that sometimes governments and organizations do conspire. He told a group at Cambridge University that it would be wrong to write off all conspiracy theorists as "swivel-eyed loons," with "poor personal hygiene and halitosis." He said that the difficult part, for those of us trying to make sense of a complex world, is working out which parts of the conspiracy theory to keep and which to throw away.[50]

TIME Magazine on the 40th anniversary of the moon landing listed ten of the world's most enduring conspiracy theories. The top ten according to TIME were the JFK Assassination; the 9/11 Cover-Up; Area 51 and the aliens; Paul

---

49 (Byers, 2015)
50 (Wheeler, 2013)

[McCartney] Is Dead; Secret Societies Control the World; the Moon Landings Were Faked; Jesus and Mary Magdalene; Holocaust Revisionism; the CIA and AIDS; and, the Reptilian Elite.[51]

Clear acts, such as terrorists on 9/11 flying planes into the World Trade Centers, are considered by some to be hoaxes. Other conspiracies are just as alarming and unsubstantiated. The dilemma is that *when people do not know what the truth is, and when they are not told the truth by the media, they are left to their imaginations*.

In late 2014 public confidence in the media, which was already low, was reported as slipping further. A poll by USA TODAY/CNN/Gallup found that only 36% of Americans believed news organizations get the facts straight.[52]

Perhaps the top conspiracy theory today is a proven lie. The Democrats, their MSM and corrupt agents in the 'Deep State' created the Trump – Russia collusion delusion in 2016. This conspiracy was based on false accusations that the Trump Administration was working with Russia during the 2016 election. It was totally made up as will be discussed later in this book.

Overall, errors in reporting by the media impact the populace's trust in the media and add to confusion and misunderstandings. As a result, Americans are more likely to believe conspiracies than they would if we had a fair and honest press.

THE MEDIA USES POLLS TO MANIPULATE

There are several ways that the truth can be distorted by the media. One way that the MSM distorts the news is to only share the stories in the news that promote their agenda whether this means stating the facts or not. Some say that this has happened much during the Obama years. Many Americans liked and voted for Obama. After his election, he could do no wrong. But the media's bias in favor of his administration made things look better than they really were.

---

51 (Time.com, n.d.)

52 (DailySource.org, 2014)

IN GOD WE TRUST

One example of media bias in recent years is in relation to public opinion polls. Television news has long been addicted to public opinion polls. Decades ago, all three broadcast networks decided to partner with an influential newspaper (ABC News with the Washington Post; CBS News with the New York Times; and NBC News with the Wall Street Journal) to sponsor their own regular surveys for use in their political coverage.[53]

What was extraordinary in 2014 was that polls used by news outlets practically vanished from the three big evening newscasts as President Obama's approval ratings tumbled, and the public opposed his administration's defining policies like Obamacare. In early September, for example, Gallup found Obama's approval rating at a record low of 38%, yet none of the three broadcast networks bothered to mention this on their evening or morning newscasts. Critics of the major media outlets suggested that such coverage was in stunning contrast to how those same newscasts relentlessly emphasized polls showing bad news for George W. Bush during the same phase of his presidency. Analysts from the Media Research Center reviewed every reference on the ABC, CBS and NBC evening newscasts to public opinion polls from January 1 through August 31, 2014, and from the same time period in 2006. In 2006 the networks aired 124 evening news reports which cited public opinion polls about either President Bush's overall approval rating or his handling of specific policies. In 2014, those same network broadcasts produced only nine reports which mentioned public opinion surveys related to President Obama.[54]

In 2006, the networks routinely highlighted Bush's falling approval ratings to illustrate his political weakness, and regularly cited polling data showing public disapproval of policies such as the Iraq war. In 2014, even as President Obama suffered his own political meltdown, the networks spared him from such coverage. The three broadcast networks conducted 15 polls asking people to rate Barack Obama's performance as President in the first three quarters of 2014 and 13 of those polls showed at least 50% of the public disapproving of how Obama handled his job. However, the three big evening newscasts in the

---

53 (Noyes, MRC Study: TV Buries the Bad News on Obama's Collapsing Polls, 2014)
54 Ibid

— 23 —

US essentially ignored their own polls, plus the dozens of others conducted by news organizations and universities that are commonly cited in routine political coverage. There were only two citations on an evening newscast of President Obama's national job approval rating. One citation on the January 28 edition of ABC's World News stated that Obama had the lowest average approval rating of any President after five years in office. Then, seven months later on the August 31 edition of the CBS Evening News, on a Sunday evening on a holiday weekend, it was noted that Democrats were facing a tough midterm election because of the President's approval rating being just above 40%. NBC's Nightly News failed to report Obama's overall approval rating during the first eight months of 2014, despite having conducted five nationwide polls on the subject.[55]

In 2006, the broadcast networks conducted 23 different polls during the first eight months that asked respondents to rank President Bush's job approval. The evening newscasts then referred to Bush's national job approval rating 52 times between January 1 and August 31 of that year, citing their own polls and surveys conducted by other organizations, as well as general characterizations of how the public regarded Bush's presidency. During this time network journalists variously described President Bush's poll numbers as "sagging," "sinking," "falling," "plummeting," "grounded," "mired," "battered," "rock bottom," at "stunning lows" and "stuck at an all-time low." It was stated in May 2006, by NBC's David Gregory that Bush's "poll ratings are now similar to Richard Nixon's when he resigned the presidency." Gregory then showed a clip of himself confronting President Bush: "Do you think it's possible that, like Nixon and Watergate, that the American people have rendered a final judgment of disapproval on you and your war in Iraq?" In 2014, President Obama faced no such coverage — no drumbeat of dour adjectives to describe his low approval ratings, and no obnoxious questions from network correspondents pleading for President Obama to participate in the drafting of his own political obituary.[56]

In 2006, over the first eight months of the year, the broadcast networks mentioned the public's rating of how the Bush administration was handling

---

55 Ibid

56 Ibid

IN GOD WE TRUST

specific policies in 90 evening news stories. On 63 occasions (70% of the time), the networks cited polling data that showed President Bush on the wrong side of public opinion on issues ranging from universal health care, the Dubai ports deal, embryonic stem cell research, immigration, gas prices, the economy and his administration's handling of the aftermath of Hurricane Katrina. In 2014, over the same time period, only four evening news reports mentioned how the public rated President Obama's handling of specific issues or policy areas. Two reports were favorable and two were unfavorable towards President Obama.[57]

Per media critics, the networks could have covered President Obama exactly as they covered President Bush eight years prior. Both Presidents were down in the polls, albatrosses to many in their parties, with the public opposed to their signature policies (Bush with Iraq and Obama with Obamacare).[58] The networks gave Obama a pass while they beat Bush to a pulp.

But the Democrats and their media have a more sinister reason for using polls. This is how they influence Americans. They do this by creating and publishing bogus polls and results and throwing them in Americans' faces. These efforts, they believe help influence peoples' behaviors because they believe everyone wants to pick a winner and if they can report that their candidate is going to win, then they hope Republicans will be discouraged and not vote.

The polls are often created to obtain the answers they want through the questions they ask. In addition, the polls select supposedly random samples that are far from random with sample sizes skewed with more Democrats than Republicans, for example.

See author Ann Coulter's best seller 'Slander' where she describes in detail how Democrats use polls to manipulate America with bogus questions and samples. This has been going on for years. Her book provides ample undisputed support related to this topic and is one of the best political books written in recent history as is evident by its sales.[59]

---

57 ibid

58 Ibid

59 (Coulter, 2003)

— 25 —

One great example of how the Democrats and their MSM used polls to pro-
mote their desired outcome occurred during the 2016 Presidential election.
Who could forget the daily barrage of polls stating Hillary was going to blow
Republican candidate Trump out of the water?

One group, Real Clear Politics, took an average of all the polls and based
on this, claimed that Hillary would be the winner. They apparently didn't realize that the polls were all slanted, ignoring the principle of 'garbage in – garbage out'.

*We didn't believe the polls either and neither did many Americans, so we made our own
prediction a few days before the election, on November 4th, 2016. We pointed out how
candidate Trump had a record setting primary and that the polls were bogus and then we
used alternative information as the basis for our prediction.*

*We reported, after being the only ones who kept track of the number of participants
at both Trump and Hillary rallies since the conventions in July, that Trump rallies accu-
mulated more than 710,000 in August through October while Hillary's only 60,000. In
August the ratio was ten to one.*

*We reported that Candidate Trump had millions more Facebook, Twitter, Instagram
and YouTube followers. Americans were viewing candidate Trump's rallies on YouTube at a
clip of three to one, for example. We also noted how signage around the States was visibly
more for Trump than Clinton and more.*

*We were right. The bogus Democrat and MSM polls were bogus. Presidential can-
didate Trump proved to the world that the slanted Democrat polls cannot be trusted.*[60]

THE MEDIA REPORTS ONLY ONE SIDE OF AN ISSUE

There are many examples of the MSM distorting the truth through only
reporting their side of the story. One example comes from late 2014 when the
unemployment results for November were released. The traditionally liberal
(pro Democratic) New York Times reported that:

---

60 (Hoft J. , Election Prediction 2016: Current Trend Lines Show Trump Will Win in
Landslide, 2016)

IN GOD WE TRUST

Ever since the recovery from the Great Recession began more than five years ago, the most crucial missing pieces of the economic puzzle were the lack of consistently strong gains in hiring and better wages for most working Americans struggling to make ends meet. Now, at last, those pieces are starting to fall into place. The Labor Department reported on Friday that employers added 321,000 jobs in November, a much stronger number than economists had predicted and the 10th consecutive month of net job gains above 200,000.[61]

The New York Times report materially differed from reports from conservative media outlets about the same Bureau of Labor Statistics (BLS) reports which reported that the labor force participation rate remained at a 36-year low of 62.8% in November. The participation rate is the percentage of the civilian non-institutional population who participated in the labor force by either having a job during the month or were actively seeking one. This rate was 62.8% in November which matched the percentage in March 1978.[62]

According to conservative news reports, in the November 2014 BLS report, the nation's civilian non-institutional population, consisting of all people 16 or older who were not in the military or an institution, reached 248,844,000, of which, 156,397,000 participated in the labor force by either holding a job or actively seeking one. The 156 million who participated in the labor force was 62.8% of the 248 million civilian non-institutional population which matched the 62.8% in April, May, June, August and October of 2014 as well as the participation rate in March of 1978. The lowest level for the participation rate in recent years was 62.7% in September 2014.[63]

The conservative accounts noted that another 92,447,000 people did not participate in the labor force, which consisted of Americans who did not have a job and were not actively trying to find one. These reports noted that when President Obama took office in January 2009, there were 80,529,000

---

61 (Schwartz, 2014)

62 (Meyer, 2014)

63 Ibid

— 27 —

Americans who were not participating in the workforce, which means that since that time, 11,918,000 Americans had left the workforce.[64] Although both the New York Times and conservative news reported facts from the same data, the stories were polar opposites regarding the state of unemployment in the US.

Gallup CEO Jim Clifton confirmed the conservative position on the level of unemployment in early February 2015 when he penned a gutsy opinion piece on Gallup's web site, defiantly calling the government's 5.6% unemployment figure "The Big Lie" in the article's headline. He then stated the next day on CNBC that he was worried he might "suddenly disappear" and not make it home for writing his comments about the real state of unemployment in the US. He too argued that the unemployment statistics in the US touted by the White House did not include those unemployed and no longer receiving unemployment or those underemployed.[65]

Today the MSM will rarely if ever report the great news in the economy. The historic stock market highs are rarely mentioned in the news. The best unemployment rates in 50 years are rarely mentioned. Historic trade deals are ignored. The destruction of evil ISIS is never mentioned. This is how the MSM attempts to control the information available to Americans.

THE MEDIA REPORTS OUTRIGHT LIES

In addition to bending the truth, or only reporting a part of a picture, sometimes the major media also distorts the truth by reporting outright lies. An example of this was pointed out by the New York Post in late 2014 about CNN's coverage of riots in Ferguson Missouri after a grand jury failed to find enough evidence to bring police officer Darren Wilson to trial for the murder of teenager Mike Brown. While the CNN cameramen from the self-proclaimed 'most trusted network', were watching cars on fire and stores being looted, the reporters rambled on about how "most people here" are "peaceful protesters."[66]

---

64 Ibid

65 (Martens, 2015)

66 (Riley, 2014)

IN GOD WE TRUST

The peaceful protesters were nowhere to be found. The reporters could not seem to find any and instead, turned to outside experts and some carefully vetted religious leaders to talk about "the real message" of the protests. Then on the ensuing Tuesday night, CNN correspondent Jason Carroll was reporting that, "Most of the protesting we saw in front of the Ferguson Police Department tonight was peaceful." He then attempted to explain the fires burning behind him, but was approached by three of the protesters, who proceeded to get in his face and yell at him because he was promoting a "certain narrative" other than their own. CNN anchor Don Lemon then quickly took the broadcast elsewhere, saying he was worried about Carroll's safety. Later in the broadcast Lemon returned to Carroll and asked him what the men were saying to him, which Carroll refused to say. The reporter was reluctant because, as he explained, these men didn't "represent" the peaceful protesters who were the real story.[67]

All that a viewer had to do was hit mute on their TV set to see the real picture of the protests. Unfortunately, there are numerous instances where the MSM outlets report a story and not the truth.

See author Ann Coulter's best seller Slander where she describes in detail numerous accounts where the left leaning media committed slander through dishonest reporting. This has been going on for years.[68]

THE MEDIA DOESN'T REPORT STORIES IT DOESN'T LIKE

Most Americans would be surprised at some of the news stories *not* reported in the major media over the past few years. For example, before the 2008 election, Barack Obama denied knowing Bill Ayers, an anti-war terrorist and confessed member of the Weather Underground group accountable for setting off bombs in the US during the Vietnam War.[69] Later it was proven that Obama did in fact know Ayers, and one argument went so far as to propose that Ayers

---

67 Ibid

68 Op cit, Coulter, Slander

69 (Griffing, 2009)

— 29 —

JOE HOFT

and Obama were so close that Ayers may have authored Obama's two books.[70] Ayers has said many derogatory things about the US. For example, as recent as 2014 he was on Iranian TV stating that the US was 'terrorist nation' and 'the greatest purveyor of violence on earth over the past half century'.[71] It is no wonder Obama tried to distance himself from Ayers and why the major media outlets have remained silent on this as well as much of Obama's past.

In 2014 it was reported that in actions similar to mobsters from the South Side of Chicago, Barack Obama and his Attorney General, Eric Holder, were seizing money from all sorts of businesses regulated under the crushing thumb of big government and then redistributing these funds to leftist organizations. Among the evidence offered for the charge of "fraud and extortion" was the intense pressure Holder's Department of Justice (DOJ), and other federal regulators put on financial institutions through fines and other settlements in the billions. The administration settled on a deal with Bank of America for $17 billion and on other deals with JP Morgan Chase and Citibank for $20 billion. The money from these banks was then funneled to hardcore progressives and other friends of the Administration to pay off delinquent debts in cities that Democrats have destroyed. Besides requiring billions in debt forgiveness payments to delinquent borrowers in Cleveland, Atlanta, Philadelphia, Oakland, Detroit, Chicago and other Democrat strongholds — and up to $500 million to cover personal taxes owed on those checks — the Bank of America deal required the bank to make billions in new loans, while also building affordable low-income rental housing in those areas. The heavily regulated financial institutions are at the government's mercy and wrote bad loans in the first place due to government regulations before the 2008 financial disaster which led to them to later being sued by the government for these same government-imposed acts in 2014.[72] This story never made MSM headlines.

If not convinced of the major media protecting the Obama Administration from being reported as engaging in shady activities, one only has to ask the

---

70 (Sessions, 2011)

71 (FNA, 2014)

72 (Rose, 2014)

— 30 —

IN GOD WE TRUST

47 Inspector Generals (IG's) who wrote to the US Congress asking for support. In 2014, 47 IG's, the officials charged with fighting corruption, waste, and wrongdoing in federal agencies, sent a letter to Congress complaining that organizations within the Federal government, ranging from the Environmental Protection Agency to the Justice Department, were impeding their investigations by withholding information. Federal law specifically forbids withholding information from the IG's, and 47 IG's comprised more than half of all such officials. Many of these IG's were appointed by President Obama himself. The IG's complained that the federal agencies they covered did not meet their requests by thwarting them, withholding documents and obstructing investigations.[73] The materiality of these irregularities, if not crimes, has not been reported adequately, if at all, by the MSM outlets. If public companies did the same to US auditors as these federal agencies, they would be indicted with multiple crimes resulting in fines and possible imprisonment as a result.

The Obama administration's foreign policy was just as shocking as its fiscal policy and most Americans never heard the full story. When Obama unilaterally started bombing Libya early in his first term in office, there was little, if any public outrage. The media for years criticized President Bush for being a war monger but gave Obama a pass with his Libya campaign. For seven months, one week and five days, Obama dropped bombs on Libya. Countless Libyan military personnel and many civilians were killed during the campaign. Obama acted without any provocation and did not seek Congressional approval to begin the bombing of Libya, a country which had not recently attacked America, and was not threatening to. There simply was no constitutional justification for Obama's unilateral bombing of Libya.[74] As a result of his actions, the US aided the terrorist organization Al Qaeda in Libya and provided them with arms in taking over the country.[75] With this action alone, the Obama administration had reversed the US's war on terror by assisting terrorists, and yet there was and has been little or no mention of this in the MSM outlets.

---

73 (Williamson, 2014)

74 (Carroll, 2014)

75 (Blog-Global-Research, 2014)

JOE HOFT

Little if any of the above stories have ever been reported by any major media outlet. These stories and numerous others are examples of the MSM not reporting stories that do not compliment the candidates they support and their left-wing agenda. The impact to the media for not reporting the facts has been a loss of readers leading to a loss in sales which has led to many news outlets closing their doors. **A news outlet may promote socialist ideas but ultimately it is capitalism that will keep the outlet in a position to continue to report and promote these ideas.**

Since 2009 the newspaper industry has been decimated. In the US more than 105 newspapers closed their doors in 2009 alone. Approximately 10,000 newspaper jobs were lost, print ad sales fell 30% and 23 of the top 25 newspapers reported circulation declines between 7% and 20%.[76] The newspapers' downward spiral continued with 151 newspaper closings in 2010 and 152 papers ceasing operations in 2011.[77] As a matter of fact, since 1990 the number of newspaper employees has plummeted while the number of Internet related employees has grown. In 1990 there were 457,800 newspaper employees. By March 2016 the number had decreased by 60% to only 183,200 employees. However, Internet employees have grown in numbers to 197,800 and have now surpassed the number of newspaper employees in the US.[78] Just like the rest, the super liberal New York Times announced in the 3rd Quarter of 2016 that they incurred a 96% decrease in quarterly profit.[79]

The television and news cable industries have seen similar results. In the third quarter of 2014, FOX News not only humiliated its leftwing cable news counterparts at CNN and MSNBC during the all-important primetime hours, FOX News also beat all of cable — all hundred or so cable channels, including perennial winners ESPN and USA in viewership. FOX News cable television channel nearly doubled the leftwing promoting networks CNN and MSNBC combined.[80] By the end of 2014, cable news channel CNBC, known for not

---

76 (Dumpala, 2009)

77 (Mendolera, 2012)

78 (Bedard, A first: More workers at online sites than newspapers, 2016)

79 (AP, 2016)

80 (Nolte, Fox News Slaughters CNN, MSNBC; Hits Historic Ratings Milestone, 2014)

— 32 —

IN GOD WE TRUST

hiding its left leaning attitude and reporting, had its lowest rated year since 1995 overall and delivered its lowest rated year ever since 1992 with the age 25-54 demographic.[81] These statistics are no mistake. They are a result of the population wanting more honesty and less bias in their news reporting.

THE MEDIA'S LINKS TO LIBERALISM

The cause of less and less people trusting the media may be related to less and less people in the media identifying themselves as Republicans. Indiana University released the results of their study in 2014 that continued a series of national studies of US journalists begun in 1971 and repeated in 1982, 1992, and 2002. The survey showed that in 2014 only 7% of the media identify themselves as Republicans. This was down from 18% of journalists who identified themselves as Republicans in 2002.[82] With statistics like these, it is no wonder that a report from GQ magazine in late December 2014 shows that 17 of the 20 politicians named in its 'Craziest Politician' list were Republicans.[83] If you look closely, you will see similar stories like these reported daily in MSM outlets like ABC, CBS, NBC, CNN, New York Times, LA Times, etc.

With such a small percent of the MSM representing one side of the political spectrum, it is not surprising that in 1998, a Gallup Poll found 52% of Republicans trusted the major news media and that in 2014, that trust level sunk to a mere 27%. And moving from distrust to bias, the Gallup poll shows 71% of Republicans believing in 2014 that the major news media is too liberal.[84]

Republican distrust with the media is not unfounded. Former CBS employee Sharyl Attkisson, wrote a memoir/exposé entitled "Stonewalled: My Fight for Truth Against the Forces of Obstruction, Intimidation, and Harassment in Obama's Washington" (Harper). In the book Attkisson unloads on her colleagues at CBS TV news for their cowardice and cheerleading for the Obama administration while she tried to unmask the corruption, misdirection and outright lying of Obama's Washington political machine. In the book she

---

81 (Durden, 2015)

82 (Weaver, 2014)

83 (O'Brien, 2014)

84 Op cit, McGlothlin

JOE HOFT

relayed many examples of liberal bias. For example, one of her bosses had a rule that conservative analysts must always be labeled conservatives, but liberal analysts were simply "analysts."[85]

It is really no surprise that Attkisson faced such opposition to stories that shed the Obama administration in a negative light. David Rhoades, the president of CBS News, is the brother of Ben Rhoades, Obama's White House national security advisor who had a major role in the editing of the now infamous Benghazi talking points. Other similar examples abound. Claire Shipman, a senior national correspondent at ABC News, is married to Jay Carney, Obama's White House Press Secretary. If the ties between the Obama White House and ABC News aren't disturbing enough, the president of ABC News, Ben Sherwood, is brother to Dr. Elizabeth Sherwood-Randall, a special advisor to Barack Obama. Another example is at CNN. Virginia Moseley is a CNN Vice President and Washington Bureau Chief and she is married to Tom Nides, a Deputy Secretary of State under Barack Obama.[86]

An article in early 2016 in the New York Times by David Samuels confirmed that senior White House officials, including Ben Rhoades, gleefully confessed that they used friendly reporters and nonprofits as public relations tools when selling President Obama's foreign policy. The White House apparently had the ability to do it almost at will because these tools "are ignorant, will believe what they're told, will essentially take dictation and are happy to be used just to get the information necessary for a tweet or two". The White House's greatest triumph, according to senior officials, was selling a misleading narrative about the nuclear deal with Iran [giving Iran $150 billion or half of Iran's GDP for Iran's promise not to build nuclear bombs]— the parameters of which were set a year before the administration claimed.[87]

---

85 (Smith, 2014)

86 (Nolte, CNN, CBS News, ABC News Honchos Have Obama Administration Family Ties, 2013)

87 (Podhoretz, 2016)

THE TRUMP YEARS – 'FAKE NEWS' BECOMES 'CORRUPT'

In September 2018, I was back in the US for a conference that my brother Jim sponsored with a group of conservative personalities and members in the media. During this same weekend I observed a media group from Denmark who came to the event and filmed Jim throughout the weekend. On Sunday morning the group was at Jim's house and they interviewed him in his kitchen. Jim said something that I had never heard before. In essence he said that there used to be a gap between the Democrat Party and the MSM. The media was far-left but they were somewhat independent and separate from the Democrat Party. What Jim then said was that this distinction is now gone. The MSM and the Democrat Party are one. Under the era of Trump, they fully joined forces and now there was no difference between the two. Jim was correct.

During the Trump years the MSM took their tricks to a level never seen before. Not only was the press totally in sync with Obama and the Hillary Clinton Campaign, they showed it and never gave candidate and President Trump a chance or a break. As a matter of fact, the MSM was so biased that they became more than purveyors of the socialist anti-American agenda, they were active participants in the hate-Trump movement.

By the end of his first year in office, the media's bias and hate of President Trump reached new highs. The Media Research Center tracked the media's coverage of President Trump in his first year in office and the results were not surprising but horrific. They wrote:

> But as the Media Research Center has been documenting all year, the media have approached the Trump presidency with unrelenting hostility. Our latest numbers show that coverage of Trump on the ABC, CBS and NBC evening newscasts in September, October and November was more than 90 percent negative (our methodology counts only explicitly evaluative statements from reporters or non-partisan sources).
>
> In September, there were just 31 pro-Trump statements on the Big Three vs. 359 negative. In October, the number of positive statements grew to 41, while the negative statements swelled to 435.

JOE HOFT

In November, there was somewhat less coverage of the President, as political journalists raced to cover the allegations against Alabama GOP Senate candidate Roy Moore, but the ratio remained essentially unchanged: 33 positive statements vs. 320 negative statements.

Add it all up, and coverage of Trump has been 91 percent negative during the past three months. Our study of news in June, July and August found an identical rate of 91% negative, which means TV news is unchanged in its hostility toward the President.[88]

The 'Deep State' was a term coined to refer to a corrupt group of individuals in the government who did all they could to prevent candidate Trump from winning the 2016 election and then did all they could to have him removed from office after he won the election. This group of individuals in the Obama Administration's FBI, DOJ, CIA and State Departments led what many believe was a coup d'etat of the Trump Presidency. These people could never have done the damage they did without a complicit MSM. The Deep State would prepare a story for the MSM which would obediently push the story through the airwaves. The stories were false, but it didn't matter. **The MSM had become one with the Democrat Party and the corrupt Deep State actors in government.**

For years this went on and on. The Deep State would create a falsehood. The MSM would report it and repeat it constantly. The story would be some sort of outrageous lie about the President of the United States, Donald Trump. The story was related to some action that the President took that was supposedly corrupt and the MSM would claim his days as President were coming to an end. We heard this over and over for three years as the MSM and the Deep State tried to connect President Trump to Russia and other absurd slanderous concoctions.

This whole time the President was under investigation by a group of Hillary-loving and Trump-hating Deep State hacks who did all they could to have the President removed from office. It was a horrible period in US history

88 (Noyes, Even As Media Whine About Trump, Their Hostile Coverage Shows No Let Up, 2017)

IN GOD WE TRUST

and especially for those who admired and voted for the President in the 2016 election. These corrupt and criminal actions ironically hardened those who voted for President Trump and increased their admiration for the President, the 'fake news' did a terrible service to the country.

President Trump became so fed up with the MSM that he suggested that he understated the media when he called them out for reporting 'fake news', no, the MSM should be more accurately referred to as 'corrupt'. Finally, the FISA report[89] was released in December 2019 that showed that the entire 'Russia Collusion' sham was based on a garbage dossier that the corrupt leaders in the FBI used to obtain FISA warrants to legitimize spying on candidate and President Trump. The Deep State FBI had lied to the court to push through the FISA warrant even though they knew in January of 2017, before President Trump's Inauguration, that the dossier was garbage and so was the FISA warrant it was based on.

The Deep State knew their entire Russia Collusion scam was based on a lie and they still pushed out their bogus lies connecting the President to Russia. In their efforts the Deep State created the Mueller Investigation, based on a lie. Instead of ending the investigation before it started because there was no evidence of any crimes committed by President Trump, Mueller and his gang harassed the President and anyone close to him for two more years. Any story that was critical of the President was promoted in the MSM. It didn't matter if the story was a complete fabrication.

In mid-December 2019 the President called out the corrupt media in a tweet:

> The Democrats and Crooked Hillary paid for & provided a Fake Dossier, with phony information gotten from foreign sources, pushed it to the corrupt media & Dirty Cops, & have now been caught. They spied on my campaign, then tried to cover it up - Just Like Watergate, but bigger![90]

---

89 (Justice, 2019)
90 (Trump, @realdonaldtrump, 2019)

The MSM after President Trump's election became so corrupt that the same individuals who perpetrated illegal activities against the President became the experts the media used to discuss the events of the day. Victor David Hansen noted this in a piece at FOX News. Hanson observed that James Comey, Andrew McCabe, John Brennan and James Clapper are former US Intel chiefs; who lied under oath or in public; who all four detest President Trump; and who are either paid cable news analysts or frequent guest commentators; then he made this observation:[91]

> In the most controversial stories, Brennan, Clapper and McCabe are being paid to analyze theories, facts and findings in which they themselves are often central players. As a guest commentator, Comey has weighed in on these controversies even as he distorts his past role in them.
>
> Yet such abject conflicts of interest are not the only ethical problems posed by these four. Until recently, all four held federal security clearances. Comey recently gave his up, apparently so he would not have to give testimony about classified information in the Horowitz investigation. The former intelligence officials sometimes gave us wink-and-nod suggestions that their television expertise was based on information not available to the general public.
>
> In sum, we are witnessing a surreal collusion between the nation's former top intelligence officials and the progressive media — beyond even the nightmares of so-called conspiracy theorists.
>
> The most powerful intelligence chiefs of the Obama administration — Brennan, Clapper, Comey and McCabe — have routinely offered the nation their own warped theories about wrongdoing in high places that are as self-serving as they are contradicted by facts.
>
> The conclusions of both the Mueller investigation and the Horowitz report are damning to the past analyses of all four.

---

91 (Hanson, 2019)

IN GOD WE TRUST

In the advocacy culture of our new media, ex-government officials such as Brennan, Clapper and McCabe can be paid to appear on news programs to analyze (or vindicate) their own unethical behavior.

As employees of the media, they sell their checkered government service to exonerate themselves while confirming the anti-Trump biases of their paying hosts.

President Trump was finally vindicated when the FISA Report was released but by this time the MSM was off on another Deep State made-up scandal, this time related to Russia's enemy, the Ukraine. Just like the first scandal, the media pushed a false narrative about the President's alleged wrong doing that was repeated over and over and eventually used as justification for the Democrats pushing through an unprecedented process to impeach President Trump for no crimes. Never mind that it was all a lie and the President did nothing wrong, the Democrats, the Deep State and their MSM declared that Trump must go.

The ties between the media and Democratic liberal politicians are endless. This is the main reason that conservatives do not feel that they are receiving accurate and unbiased news coverage in the media. This is because the MSM is the marketing arm of the Democrat Party.

Conservatives have the policies that make sense, and an honest media alternative has evolved which is more powerful than the MSM – the 'New Media'.

NEW MEDIA IS THE ANSWER

Websites like my brother Jim Hoft's thegatewaypundit.com get more than 30 million hits a month and are now competing with the legacy liberal MSM outlets. These and other relatively new large and fast-growing websites are challenging the MSM in content, objectiveness and readership. Liberal Democrats and MSM agencies and outlets have noticed and are trying to replicate and prevent the new media growth and circulation.

— 39 —

'New media' refers to the increasing number of online Internet sites and individuals who report news via the web, Twitter, Facebook, and any other kind of social media. These news services, Internet sites and blogs are increasing in power and in number and are challenging almost every report made by the old main stream media today. Most of these entities have start dates after 2000 shortly after the advent of the Internet.

"For years, America's left-leaning MSM outlets have belittled and rebuked members of the new media — questioning their credibility, impugning their integrity and assigning all manner of self-serving motivations to their contributions to the marketplace of ideas."[92] This clearly is because of the threat that new media is to the major media outlets in the US.

New media is quicker in reporting a story. When a story occurs, new media is on it. With the use of Twitter, Facebook and the Internet, fresh stories in the new media are old news by the time the nightly news show and morning papers arrive. *The new media is also more accurate* due to the many users and reporters of events. When a story is first lodged on the Internet is spreads like wildfire and any rebukes are addressed almost immediately, ending in more accurate and timely news.

As far as the credibility of the new media, one recent story involving Obamacare is an eye-opening example. In April 2011 reporter Matthew Boyle of The Daily Caller (new media) website published a report outlining the details of Barack Obama's socialized medicine slush fund:

> Boyle's report — like hundreds of investigative pieces published every day by new media outlets — was in and of itself a rebuke of many of the criticisms leveled against Internet journalists by the legacy press. Not only did Boyle accurately relate new primary source material — including excerpts from public documents and Congressional testimony — but he also sought, received and published the response of those with conflicting views regarding this information. On top of that, he presented the facts sans any editorial commentary. In other words, Boyle's investigative

---

92 (Rich, 2011)

IN GOD WE TRUST

report was every bit as "pure" journalistically as something you would read in The Washington Post or watch on the CBS Evening News.[93]

Boyle reported that two old media left leaning giants, the Washington Post and CBS, received hundreds of thousands of dollars from the Early Retiree Reinsurance Program (ERRP), an Obamacare slush fund that arbitrarily doled out nearly $2 billion to select corporations, government pension funds and labor unions between 2010 and 2011. This fund was created by the Obama Administration as a means of protecting health care coverage prior to the onset of the socialized medicine law and was rife with corruption and mismanagement — as evidenced by payments to media outlets that were supposed to objectively cover Obamacare.[94]

The MSM wrote very little about ERRP. A follow-up report on the website Hot Air revealed that both The Washington Post and CBS completely ignored problems with the slush fund secretly bankrolling health care for its early retirees. According to Hot Air, a search for ERRP on The Washington Post website and on CBS's websites, revealed nothing. A search for the full name of the slush fund revealed only one article on the Post website (a column that referenced a new media report, ironically) and on CBS's website returned only one entry, a link to the Obama administration's health care reform website.[95]

American poet Ella Wheeler Wilcox wrote that **"to sin by silence when we should protest makes cowards of men."** The same can be applied to the media, too — although a compelling case could be made that these MSM outlets were paid for their silence. "Fortunately for taxpayers, the new media was there to uncover and expose the truth regarding this corruption."[96]

CONTROLLING INTERNET AND SOCIAL MEDIA
Because 'new media' poses such a threat to those in the legacy 'old media', legislation in the Obama Administration was in the works to control the new

---

93 Ibid

94 Ibid

95 Ibid

96 Ibid

— 41 —

media and subsequently prevent the old legacy media from losing its strangle hold on the information provided to US citizens. In early February of 2015, both of the Obama Administration's Federal Communications Commission (FCC) and Federal Election Commission (FEC) declared their intention to regulate the Internet. As author and radio host Tammy Bruce wrote, "Fascists always explain their actions as efforts to either make something more efficient, "fair," or to supposedly "protect" their target. Sometimes they simply lie, like saying they're nationalizing health insurance to make it more affordable and to increase access to health care."[97]

Bruce went on to state that the legacy or old media have swamped newspapers and the broadcast networks with left leaning "true believers" who have created nothing more than PR agencies for the leftist agenda.[98]

> But now they want more. The left's relevance relies on controlling the public discussion. Bill Clinton learned of the Internet's importance when the legacy media, via Newsweek, "held the [Monica Lewinsky] story" according to Michael Isikoff, their reporter at the time, in comments reported by the Weekly Standard.
>
> Then some guy with a website called "Drudge" made sure the American people were informed about the reckless actions of a self-obsessed president.[99]

Obama's FCC Chairman Tom Wheeler announced that the FCC was claiming the power on the Internet like that of a utility service and as a result the FCC would regulate Internet service providers and the speed rate at which they provide Internet service. Of course, this would be done to make the Internet "fairer". But the truth of the matter is that Mr. Wheeler kept his 332-page document outlining his plan secret from the American public. Instead, he only released a four-page summary with major points, while refusing to release the full document.[100]

---

97 (Bruce, 2015)

98 Ibid

99 Ibid

100 Ibid

IN GOD WE TRUST

In response to the proposed FCC law, fellow FCC Commissioner Ajit Pai said that the American people were being misled about President Obama's plan to regulate the Internet. He stated that he had read the 332-page plan and it was worse than imagined with reclassifications for broadband that would open the door to taxes and onerous regulations and give the FCC "broad and unprecedented discretion to micromanage the Internet."[101]

Next, as the Washington Examiner reported, it was the FEC's turn to attack free speech as Democrats on the Commission signaled that they were prepared to forge ahead with new regulations on bloggers and others using the Internet to support candidates and influence public policy. This move reversed a 2006 decision to keep the agency's hands off the Internet. The Chairman of the FEC, Ann Ravel, had said publicly before this news was released that she wanted to control political information on the Internet.[102]

President Obama, believing that giving the FCC power to control the Internet was not enough, in late 2016 decided to use his powers to surrender the oversight of the Internet from the US to an obscure non-profit called the Internet Association for Assigned Names and Numbers, ICANN. The Internet for years was governed by the US but this action moved the overseer rights to the non-for-profit ICANN. The problem with this according to the late Phyllis Schlafly was that Obama's plan was "like telling the fox to guard the chicken coop," trusting the likes of Cuba, Venezuela and China to ensure the continued freedom of the Web. Schlafly said that this might be most dangerous use yet of Obama's executive orders. It essentially moved for no reason Internet oversight to ICANN so that rogue regimes could have the power to influence the Internet in ways that will prevent free speech and burden Internet business unrelentingly.[103]

Despite a court case asking that Obama's move to give the Internet away produced by four states in late September 2016, an Obama appointed judge stepped in and refused to prevent Obama's give away on October 1st 2016.

---

101 Ibid

102 Ibid

103 (Unruh, 2016)

— 43 —

ICANN became able to charge excessive fees on users and ultimately set mandates on who can use the Internet. This used to be overseen by the US government. The only reason imaginable for Obama to do this is to prevent the super successful conservative voice on the Internet from being heard.

STOPPING SOCIAL MEDIA'S ATTACKS AGAINST CONSERVATIVES

After Donald Trump's win in the 2016 Presidential election, the elites and liberals knew they had to make changes to social media which was given credit for Trump's win. The liberal media complex owned the periodicals, newspapers and major TV and cable TV news channels and therefore owned the messages which bashed Trump non-stop 24 hours a day. With the constant barrage from these left-wing outlets calling Trump all sorts of names and spreading the message that Trump would be so terrible for the county, how did Trump win the election? Trump won the election due to alternative information sources available through social media and through the Internet.

Immediately after the 2016 election, the Democrats went into a rage trying to figure out how their candidate Hillary Clinton could have lost to candidate Trump. They cried, shared, bitched and contemplated their loss. Eventually they went to work attempting to define how they lost the election while looking for a way to prevent it from happening again.

By early March of 2017 the left had put together their findings. The Columbia Journalism Review produced a report based on an exhaustive study to determine how Hillary could have possibly lost the 2016 election.[104] The study noted that many blamed Russian interference and 'fake news' (the term coined by Obama but quickly flipped and picked up by President-elect Trump to describe the legacy media.) Then the study went on to report the following:

> We have a less exotic, but perhaps more disconcerting explanation: Our own study of over 1.25 million stories published online between April 1, 2015 and Election Day shows that a right-wing media network

---

104 (Yochai Benkler, 2017)

IN GOD WE TRUST

anchored around Breitbart developed as a distinct and insulated media system, using social media as a backbone to transmit a hyper-partisan perspective to the world. This pro-Trump media sphere appears to have not only successfully set the agenda for the conservative media sphere, but also strongly influenced the broader media agenda, in particular coverage of Hillary Clinton.

While concerns about political and media polarization online are longstanding, our study suggests that polarization was asymmetric. Pro-Clinton audiences were highly attentive to traditional media outlets, which continued to be the most prominent outlets across the public sphere, alongside more left-oriented online sites. But pro-Trump audiences paid the majority of their attention to polarized outlets that have developed recently, many of them only since the 2008 election season.

Attacks on the integrity and professionalism of opposing media were also a central theme of right-wing media. Rather than "fake news" in the sense of wholly fabricated falsities, many of the most-shared stories can more accurately be understood as disinformation: the purposeful construction of true or partly true bits of information into a message that is, at its core, misleading. Over the course of the election, this turned the right-wing media system into an internally coherent, relatively insulated knowledge community, reinforcing the shared worldview of readers and shielding them from journalism that challenged it. The prevalence of such material has created an environment in which the President can tell supporters about events in Sweden that never happened, or a presidential advisor can reference a non-existent "Bowling Green massacre."

[*Note that this study picked two virtually unreported stories as examples of fake news. The study obviously never addressed Hillary's health issues that went virtually unreported in the MSM, the Clinton Foundation scandals, and other issues only reported in new media, let alone the constant pro-Hillary – anti-Trump propaganda in the MSM daily.*]

We began to study this ecosystem by looking at the landscape of what sites people share. If a person shares a link from Breitbart, is he or she more likely also to share a link from Fox News or from

— 45 —

The New York Times? We analyzed hyperlinking patterns, social media sharing patterns on Facebook and Twitter, and topic and language patterns in the content of the 1.25 million stories, published by 25,000 sources over the course of the election, using Media Cloud, an open-source platform for studying media ecosystems developed by Harvard's Berkman Klein Center for Internet & Society and MIT's Center for Civic Media.

When we map media sources this way, we see that Breitbart became the center of a distinct right-wing media ecosystem, surrounded by Fox News, the Daily Caller, the Gateway Pundit, the Washington Examiner, Infowars, Conservative Treehouse, and Truthfeed.

[The Columbia Journalism Review went on to share the top entities that were retweeted and shared on Facebook before the election. The list included the Gateway Pundit rated fourth in the list of most influential conservative media outlets before the 2016 election:]

@realDonaldTrump retweeters	@HillaryClinton retweeters
Breitbart	Washington Post
The Hill	Huffington Post
Fox News	New York Times
Gateway Pundit	The Hill
Politico	CNN
Washington Examiner	Politico
Daily Caller	Politicus USA
CNN	Daily Kos
Washington Post	Raw Story
New York Times	hillaryclinton.com
donaldjtrump.com	MSNBC
Conservative Treehouse	Salon
Infowars	Think Progress
Daily Mail	Daily Newsbin
Truthfeed	Mother Jones
New York Post	Talking Points Memo
Investors	Daily Beast
The Right Scoop	Media Matters
statespoll.com	NBC News
Conservative Tribune	Vox

IN GOD WE TRUST

The Democrats and their media had found the sinister reason for their loss. It was not biased or untrue reporting on their part. It was not that they had a horrible candidate who was preordained by the liberal elite establishment to become the 45th President of the United States. It was because, per the Columbia Journalism Review:

Facebook and Twitter certainly enabled right-wing media to circumvent the gatekeeping power of traditional media.[105]

The Democrats and their media acknowledged that these gatekeeper usurpers must be stopped! And this is precisely what they have attempted to do. One by one over the three years after the 2016 election, the social media giants began their attack on conservative thought.

The socials took three major steps in their efforts to destroy conservative media.

1. The Socials first action was to prevent any conservative messages from being shared on their platforms.
Behind people's backs the socials stopped conservative related posts, like those from the Gateway Pundit, from being shared. Individuals on Twitter or Facebook might think they were sharing Gateway Pundit posts with their friends, but they were not. Twitter and Facebook created algorithms that prevented posts from entities like the Gateway Pundit from being shared. Individuals might think their friends or followers were seeing their shares and tweets, but they were not. The socials prevented them from being shared. (Note that Facebook and Twitter have never shared these algorithms with the public and this lack of transparency feeds the negative view of these new media platforms.)

Next the socials created a group of gatekeepers. Far-left agencies and entities were selected to be these gatekeepers. Any posts or messages that the

---

105 Ibid

socials didn't like based on these 'independent' entities was labeled as 'fake news' and the posts were taken down or not shared.

It is not uncommon to see a conservative voice removed from these platforms for no reason other than they are extremely popular and have huge followings. Individuals like actor and conservative James Woods and conservative firebrand Alex Jones and his entity Info Wars were all banned by the social zealots. History will show these actions by the Socials be in line with the actions of Nazi Germany and Communist China.

These actions from the socials place them in the most precarious situation. If they are publishers, then they can sued for posts shared on their sites, so they claim to be something else. But if they are not publishers then they have no right to prevent conservative tweets and posts from being shared their sites. They either are publishers, or they are not but they cannot be both. **This needs to be addressed quickly, but unfortunately Democrats in the US House and Senate like things the way they are, and Republican leadership seems to have no idea what is going on!**

2. The Socials prevented conservative articles from being viewed via Google searches

Dr. Robert Epstein reported in 2018 that Google searches impacted the 2016 election significantly. Dr. Epstein calculates that by configuring the results of searches on Google, the company was able to impact election decisions. For example, if someone was to query taxes or economy, the results in the Google searches would be towards liberal MSM outlets and stories that promoted Hillary Clinton and denigrated candidate Trump. By setting up its searches in this manner, Dr. Epstein estimated that Hillary Clinton gained between 2 million and 10.4 million votes in the 2016 election without anybody even knowing.[106]

Epstein said people searching Google for politically relevant or election-related information will see search suggestions pop up as they

---

106 (Creitz, 2019)

IN GOD WE TRUST

type, and also see a number of top searches on the first page of their results. He claimed the alleged bias manifested itself largely within those two areas.

"We now know that those search suggestions have a very, very powerful effect on people and that they alone can shift opinions and votes dramatically and then search results appear below," he said.

"The point is if there's a bias in them -- which means if a search result that's high up on the list, if that takes you to a web page that makes one candidate look better than another -- if you're undecided and you're trying to make up your mind, what we've learned is that information posted high in Google search results will shift opinions among undecided people dramatically because people trust Google." [107]

Google also owns YouTube and does the same with that platform. Numerous conservatives have also reported having their sites on YouTube demonetized or even shut down. This is happening across the various social media platforms.

3. The socials prevented conservative websites from earning advertising dollars equal to the left-wing 'fake news' sites

This topic rarely, if ever, gets mentioned when the biased actions of social media are discussed but the results are just as devastating for conservative media outlets. Facebook and Google control a very large percent of ads that are displayed on the Internet. One report in 2019 shared the following:[108]

The U.S. internet advertising industry is projected to hit $160 billion by 2023 from $107 billion last year, led by fast-growing categories like mobile video with Alphabet Inc's Google and Facebook Inc firmly controlling the market, consultancy PwC said on Wednesday.

The two tech giants together commanded nearly 60% of the U.S. internet advertising market in 2018, according to the report, up 3%

---

107 Ibid

108 (Dang, 2019)

— 49 —

from the previous year. Google's YouTube dominates online video, while Facebook has been expanding its video product called Watch and adding advertising options.

Google and Facebook are both currently under watch by U.S. regulators for possible antitrust concerns, as well as tech giants Apple Inc and Amazon.com Inc.

Facebook and Google basically own the massive web ad market. The problem with this for any websites, especially conservative writers and websites, is that if these very large and powerful entities determine that they want to ban you and your site, they can basically shut you down.

A typical website receives ad revenue from web ads from these oligopolies. The amount paid to the website is based on the number of hits and the amount of revenue per hit. If all things were even, the larger websites would receive more revenues because they have more hits. Again, more hits equal more income. Those small web ads can pay handsomely if a website receives a healthy amount of traffic.

The problem is Google and Facebook can decide that they don't want their ads on your website. This clearly impacts revenues for the sites that are shunned and that is exactly what they have done. Facebook and Google have determined that they no longer wish to place ads on certain websites and this basically has ended the financial viability of these sites and they have had to shut down.

Google and Facebook can also pay less at certain sites per hit. This too is a way that the Socials can discriminate against conservative, pro-Trump messages that they do not like or wish to support. This is a very important activity that is going on that most Americans have no clue about and it's discriminatory and unjust.

A CASE STUDY: THE GATEWAY PUNDIT

My brother Jim started his blog — now website — years ago. He wanted to report the truth and saw in the early 2000's that the MSM was not reporting the truth. After years of

IN GOD WE TRUST

posts daily he saw his site grow from a few followers to millions. Jim posted the following on July 17, 2018, at his Gateway Pundit website:[109]

In 2017 Harvard and Columbia Journalism Review found that The Gateway Pundit was the 4th most influential conservative news source in the 2016 election.

Because of this we were targeted and have seen our numbers related to Facebook and Twitter decline dramatically.

In every single Facebook category our numbers are down. In page visits our numbers were skyrocketing before the election. Then in three distinct periods our numbers were cut off. This had nothing to do with the quality of our posts as we have proof that our generic numbers are up and continue to increase.

In all statistical categories provided to us by Facebook our current numbers are below linear projections of where we should be.

In February, Facebook launched another algorithm change to their platform. With the changes we saw our traffic dwindle even further.

We weren't the only ones to be affected. The algorithmic change caused President Donald Trump's engagement on Facebook posts to plummet a whopping 45%.

In contrast, according to Breitbart's Allum Bokhari, Senators Elizabeth Warren (D-MA) and Bernie Sanders (I-VT) do not appear to have suffered a comparable decline in Facebook engagement.

This is a criminal act. Facebook took our money for advertising and promised a fair playing field. Facebook lied to us and every conservative group in America.

Today despite the fact that we have 635,000 Gateway Pundit Facebook fans. We receive almost nothing from Facebook. [The Gateway Pundit in early 2020 regularly has more than a million page views a day.]

---

109 (Hoft J. , SHOCK STUDY: Facebook Has Eliminated 93% of Traffic to Top Conservative Websites Since 2016 Election, 2018)

JOE HOFT

Facebook is doing this to a number of top conservative sites we are in contact with. A recent Pew Study found that 71% of Americans see how tech giants are censoring political content.

And now this...

A Gateway Pundit June study of top conservative news outlets found that Facebook has eliminated 93% of traffic to top conservative websites. Facebook began eliminating conservative content after the 2016 election.

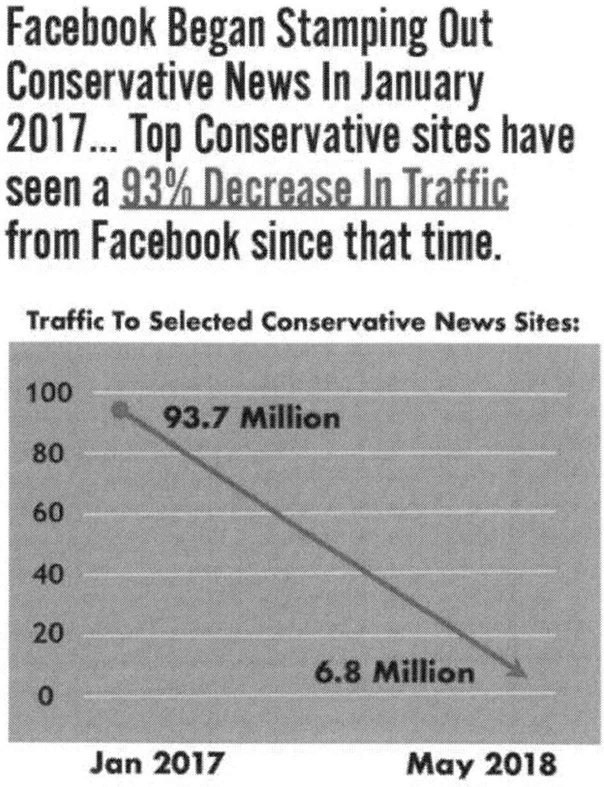

Facebook Began Stamping Out Conservative News In January 2017... Top Conservative sites have seen a 93% Decrease In Traffic from Facebook since that time.

Traffic To Selected Conservative News Sites:

93.7 Million

6.8 Million

Jan 2017   May 2018

Jim later was invited to speak in front of the Subcommittee on the Constitution and Social Justice in Congress in September 2018, about the actions that are currently taking place against conservatives by the Social media giants. Here is an excerpt from his presentation:

IN GOD WE TRUST

The Gateway Pundit business cultivated its audience on Facebook, spending roughly $70,000 advertising on Facebook in 2015 resulting in 600,000 Facebook likes and supporters.

Over the past 19 months, Gateway Pundit saw a decline in our Facebook traffic from 24% of total website traffic in January 2017 to 2% of total website traffic in June 2018. This is an 88% decrease in traffic from Facebook.

Recently we analyzed traffic numbers for some of the top conservative publishers in the U.S. What we found was simply shocking. Just as Gateway Pundit had been eliminated by Facebook from being seen by its readers, Facebook eliminated 93% of combined referral traffic to these websites from January 2017 to May 2018.

The site Western Journal and other conservative websites under their umbrella had more than a billion page views in 2016. Since then the organization lost 75% of its Facebook traffic. Likewise, Klicked Media, host of over 60 conservative websites, lost 400 million page views from Facebook in the last six months when compared to the prior year. The total number of pageviews lost by just these two conservative online publishers is more than 1.5 billion pageviews from Facebook in one year.

After the 2016 election, Facebook began making algorithm changes to ensure conservative news was no longer an option for their users. Two studies released in March of 2018 confirm this. A study by The Outline Organization found conservative publishers were hit the hardest by recent Facebook algorithm changes — and that The Gateway Pundit was hit the hardest.

A Western Journal study in March revealed the same startling statistics. Further, this study found that liberal publishers actually saw a 2 percent increase in traffic.

In fact, we found that every prominent conservative website from 2016 has either had their Facebook traffic diminished or entirely eliminated.

If Facebook were seeking to hold a book burning, they wouldn't have been half as successful as they were in eliminating contrary points of view from being accessed by the American people.

— 53 —

(The full presentation can be found in Appendix I at the end of this book.)

Liberals realize they cannot win elections when information is based on the truth, so they are doing all they can to control information being shared with Americans on the Internet. Liberals hate free speech.

After the 2016 election, President Obama started a campaign that labeled conservative websites that shared the truth about events surrounding the 2016 election 'Fake News'. In line with Obama, Google and Facebook announced that they would begin limiting the number of advertisements that these 'Fake News' sites could display on their sites, therefore hitting these sites in the pocketbook.[110] These efforts along with liberal overlords taking over the Internet are intent on shutting down free speech.

Americans are the last line of defense against the US government and corrupt nations from taking over the Internet and removing one of the remaining elements of free speech left in America.

The freedom of the Internet has made it incredibly attractive and universal. It was created with a utilitarian approach to be used everywhere by everyone for free. It must stay this way.

Regrettably for Americans, the old legacy media is not reporting on issues honestly and as instantaneously as the new media. It is against the old media's mission to do so. Providentially, there are books, some politicians, some media outlets and the new media of Internet sites and blogs which are revitalizing the virtues of the press and are quickly becoming the news medium of the future. These entities are showing that the truth is what matters most to Americans and that Americans, like others throughout history, are willing to work to find the truth.

The Soviet experience shows that when the state runs the media the information provided to its populous is more propaganda than unbiased information. In situations like these the truth is lost and craved for. In Russia during the Cold War years, the samizdat, or underground press, and Radio Free Europe

---

110 (Cooke, 2016)

IN GOD WE TRUST

provided an alternative to the state-run media monopoly by refuting the disinformation coming from the media. The blogosphere has become the samizdat in the US today. "The only gateway for the press in a free republic must be that of stand-alone fact."[111] New media supplies the facts necessary for Americans to make informed decisions. Let us hope, pray and do all we can to ensure that the new media continues to prosper, and the Internet continues to be free.

Americans must fight to keep the Internet and social media free and then promote and use the many 'new media' alternatives available today that endorse reporting of the facts while confronting the legacy media's 'fake news'. The government must step in to protect freedom of speech. Finally, Republicans need to wake up because if the current group of Democrats get in power they will prevent conservative speech from being shared for eternity (they are already more than half way there).

---

111 Op cit, Henley, 2012

3

TRUTH AND HONESTY
FROM OUR POLITICIANS

LIKE THE LACK of trust in the media, the US faces a crisis in its lack of trust in its politicians. In 2014, polls of both President Obama and Congress showed them held in low esteem by most Americans. Perhaps politicians are not to be trusted because the media lets them get away with so much? Whatever the reason, still today trust in American politicians is at rock bottom. This is one reason why President Trump won the 2016 election. He was an outsider.

In October of 2014, one month before the midterm elections, President Obama's approval rating was at a presidential 16 year low. The Gallup polling agency measures presidential approval ratings and found that Obama's approval rating was lower than both Clinton and Bush and had not been so low since President Clinton's rating in 1998 when he was in the process of being impeached for lying about having sex with an intern.[112]

The US Congress was as unpopular as President Obama. In the mid-term elections held in November 2014 the Democrats representing Obama's party were badly beaten as Republicans gained the majority in the Senate and gained

---

112 (Bedard, Gallup: Voter opposition to Obama at 16-year high, worse than Bush, Clinton, 2014)

IN GOD WE TRUST

additional seats in the House. However, even after the big gains most Republican voters felt that the leaders of both parties were working for special interests and that the ordinary people had no say in the government. Republican voters were highly dissatisfied with the direction of the country and with President Obama, and pessimistic about the economy. But Republican dissatisfaction had no partisan boundaries as support for the Republican leaders in Congress was surprisingly low among these Republican voters as well.[113]

The largest concern of Americans in 2014 was the problem with American politicians according to one Gallup poll. Four issues were identified as the nation's most important problems, with complaints about government leadership, including President Barack Obama and the Republicans in Congress and the general political conflict, leading the list at 18%. This problem was closely followed by the economy in general (17%), unemployment or jobs (15%) and healthcare (10%).[114]

A poll released in April of 2014 confirmed that a majority of voters viewed the perpetually expanding Leviathan of the US Federal Government as a threat to individual rights and individual liberty. More than a third of Americans feared the federal government, the poll showed, confirming other surveys finding broad public agreement that Washington, D.C., had become dangerous and out of control.

The Rasmussen Reports national survey also showed that trust in federal authorities was plunging fast. More than two thirds of voters polled, said they viewed the federal government as a special interest group primarily concerned with protecting its own interests. Majorities of Republicans, Democrats, and independents all agreed with this finding. Less than 20% of Americans surveyed trusted the Washington-based political and bureaucratic classes to do the right thing most of the time and 36% of voters surveyed said the federal government rarely or never does the right thing.[115]

---

113 (Moore, 2015)

114 (Saad, 2015)

115 (Newman, 2014)

Those in the American military were also fed up with US politicians. In December 2014 a poll by the *Military Times* newspaper of some 2,300 active-duty service members concluded that Obama's popularity had crumbled, falling from 35% in 2009 to just 15% in 2014, while his disapproval ratings increased to 55% from 40% in 2009. Obama's poor results came from military members who believed he had an inconsistent and flawed foreign policy. Obama's 2011 removal of all troops in Iraq for example, helped lead to the rise of the Islamic State which led to a new US intervention in the region. Some additional resistance came from those who saw Obama changing the military through heavy-handed social engineering that eroded deep-seated traditions and potentially undermined good order and discipline.[116]

Obama is not the only politician who has suffered in the *Military Times* poll. There was an increasing disillusionment with both political parties, and those service members who considered themselves Republicans slowly dropped from nearly half of those surveyed to just 32% in 2014. The poll noted that increasingly, the newspaper's readers are more likely to describe themselves as libertarian (7%) or independent (28%) with Democrats and liberals making up some 8% of the poll respondents.[117]

POLITICIANS ARE ABOVE THE LAW

One reason that politicians are so despised is that some politicians feel that they are above the law. A recent example of a government employee acting in a manner where she was above the law was the recent email scandal involving former Secretary of State Hillary Clinton. Mrs. Clinton was the US Secretary of State during President Obama's first term in office. She is the wife of former President Bill Clinton and the former US Senator from New York. After her husband served his second term, Mrs. Clinton ran as a Democrat and won the US Senate race in New York. Then in 2008, Mrs. Clinton ran for President and lost to Barack Obama. After winning the Presidency, Obama offered Mrs. Clinton the Secretary of State position in his administration. An email

---

116 (Fund, 2014)

117 Ibid

IN GOD WE TRUST

scandal involving Mrs. Clinton originated as a result of her four-year stint in this position.

In March 2015 it was reported that Hillary Clinton maintained her work emails during her role as Secretary of State on her own personal email server. This came as a surprise at the time because the State Department for years told underlings not to use personal email for official government business. A 2011 State Department cable, sent to diplomatic and consular staff in June 2011 and bearing Clinton's electronic signature, made clear to employees they were expected to "avoid conducting official Department business from your personal e-mail accounts." The message also said employees should not "auto-forward Department email to personal email accounts which is prohibited by Department policy". Mrs. Clinton ignored her own advice.[118]

In July 2015 the New York Times reported that two inspectors general had asked the US Justice Department to open an investigation into whether sensitive government information was mishandled in connection with the personal email account Mrs. Clinton used as Secretary of State. The request was made after an assessment in June 2015 by the inspectors general for the State Department and the intelligence agencies that Mrs. Clinton's private account contained hundreds of potentially classified emails. Mrs. Clinton who was again running for President, repeatedly stated that she had no classified information on the account after her use of a private email account for official State Department business was revealed in March 2015.[119]

After months of speculation and a material negative impact on her second Presidential campaign, Mrs. Clinton went on a Sunday show to discuss her email situation. She first was asked why she went through the time and effort to maintain her work emails on her own home server. This was never really answered. Even the casual observer would wonder why someone would have their own setup unless they had something to hide. Next, she was asked about why the emails were requested in the first place. Mrs. Clinton answered this query stating that there were many requests for the information and the State

---

118 (Herridge, 2015)
119 (Apuzzo, 2015)

— 59 —

Department had 'record keeping issues' not noting that the 'State Department' was her department at the time for when the emails were being requested. Mrs. Clinton was also asked about a discrepancy with one of her prior claims. Mrs. Clinton previously made a statement under oath that all her records had been turned over, but a chain of emails with US General Petraeus were subsequently discovered that she had not turned over.[120]

Mrs. Clinton made numerous false statements surrounding her emails. In March 2015 she made the excuse that the reason she used a personal e-mail address for official business as Secretary of State was so that all her e-mails came to one device. However, a few weeks later it was uncovered that Mrs. Clinton used more than one device for her emails. She also said that her personal server contained personal emails from her husband, the former President, and herself. However, this too was debunked after a former Clinton aide said that the former President had only sent out two emails in his entire life. She also said that she had never emailed any classified information using her personal email account and after a small sample was taken of her emails, this too turned out false. Finally, after months of resisting, Clinton agreed to hand over her home server to the FBI. Unfortunately, the server had been totally wiped clean.[121]

One reason that the emails were requested was that Congress was trying to ascertain her actions before and after the murder of four Americans in the US Consulate in Benghazi, Libya. When the four Americans were killed, including the US Ambassador, the immediate response from Clinton's State Department and the Obama Administration was that the cause of the event was a reaction to a video by an American in the US which presented Islam in a derogatory context. After this was proven questionable at best, investigations ensued as to why the false narrative would be pushed in the first place and what was really going on in Benghazi as well as why those calling for assistance that terrible night were denied any US backing.

Information was requested from Mrs. Clinton and it was learned that her emails were all on her personal server. Mrs. Clinton did not allow any agencies to

---

120 (Shaw, 2015)

121 (Board, 2015)

IN GOD WE TRUST

obtain access to the servers where she housed her work emails, she instead said that she supplied all emails related to the requests and implied that she should be trusted that the list was complete. Any novice auditor or investigator would know that something was wrong if an individual being audited or investigated did not provide full access to any data or system being investigated. In addition, when a sample of emails was reviewed and any of the emails were found to be classified after being told that they were not, an additional sample and more robust review would ensue.

In addition, any individuals with government experience with top secret information could tell you that they are repeatedly reminded to take good care of the information that they have or have seen to ensure it is well protected. This is repeated over and over. Someone with the security clearance like the one Mrs. Clinton had while Secretary of State would have surely known that classified information was to be maintained on government servers and that any information even remotely classified should be handled with care and be confined to well-protected environments, like government servers. The fact that Mrs. Clinton even decided to house government related emails on her personal server was incomprehensible. She eventually destroyed phones with a hammer that were requested as part of her email investigation. This whole debacle is one example why Americans' distrust politicians.

POLITICIANS AND MONEY

Another big reason that Americans do not trust their politicians is due to the manner that they are voted in and what they do as soon as they win their elections. No sooner do they get elected, and they begin running on their next campaign and this means they are busy fundraising. It is estimated that politicians in Washington D.C. spend between 30% and 70% of their time fundraising. A politician needs money to run a campaign and pay for advertising in various media outlets and as a result, much of their time is spent in sending out fundraising letters, collecting small checks in the mail, online or at a local public event. However, most of their fundraising time is spent in Washington D.C. attending private fundraising events.[122]

---

122 (Schweizer, 2013, p. 58)

— 61 —

US Congressional fundraising has remained constant throughout the years whether it is an election year or not. For example, in 2011 which is an off year for elections, congressional representatives and senators held more than 2,841 fundraisers in the nation's capital. Politicians make hundreds of phone calls between votes, meetings and nightly fundraising receptions.[123] This is the work they do to stay in power. The government created a democracy but what has evolved is more like a multifaceted money grabbing machine.

Politicians spend time fundraising because this helps them win elections. There is no guarantee of course that the biggest spenders win elections, as President Trump showed in the 2016 Presidential election. There are numerous cases where wealthy candidates lose elections. However, statistics show that money does matter. In nine out of ten House of Representatives elections and in eight out of ten Senate races, the candidate who spends the most money wins.[124] The overall challenge that Americans have with fundraising is that there is the potential for individuals or entities to 'buy' a vote or influence legislation based on money and not what is good for the people.

One unique example of a fundraising scheme of sorts was created by the Clintons. After President Clinton had left office, the Clinton Foundation was created. This entity was set up as a non-profit organization which means it does not have to pay taxes that for-profit corporations have to pay. According to its website, the Clinton Foundation is an operating foundation. The money raised by the Foundation is spent directly on its programs, and not as grants to other charitable organizations. Most of the Clinton Foundation's charitable work is performed and implemented by its staff and partners on the ground. The Foundation states that it operates programs around the world that have a significant impact in a wide range of issue areas, including economic development, climate change, health and wellness, and participation of girls and women.[125] (It is not exactly clear what the 'participation of girls and women' means since President Clinton was impeached and disbarred due to lying about

---

123 Ibid, p. 58-59.

124 Ibid, p. 61.

125 (Foundation, n.d.)

IN GOD WE TRUST

sexual relations with women when under oath in a sexual harassment lawsuit against him.)

In April 2015 it was reported on Bloomberg that that the Clinton Foundation refused to disclose the identities of at least 1,100 donors, most of whom are not U.S. citizens, to a Clinton Foundation affiliate. "The donations were routed through the Clinton Giustra Enterprise Partnership (Canada), or CGEPartnership, a Canadian charitable organization. That organization then effectively bundled the foreign donations and sent them along to the Clinton Foundation itself, and it did all of this without ever disclosing the individual foreign sources of the income. If that sounds to you like more of a laundering operation than a charitable organization, that's because it certainly looks like more of a laundering operation than a charitable organization."[126]

The traditionally liberal (Democrat leaning) New York Times (shockingly) released the story about the Clinton's shady acts with wealthy individuals. The authors first uncovered connections between a uranium mining magnate by the name of Frank Giustra, his Canadian charitable organization, the Clinton Foundation, and official actions taken by Secretary of State Hillary Clinton that benefitted Giustra's global uranium mining operations. After this was reported, the Clinton Foundation immediately entered spin mode. Foundation executives stated when this story was released that the Canadian CGEPartnership was banned by federal law in Canada from releasing any donor names without the prior consent of the donor. This sounded reasonable until *The Federalist* found that the Clinton Foundation's claim had zero merit. Multiple Canadian tax and privacy law experts contacted by *The Federalist* stated that there was no such blanket prohibition on public disclosure of charitable donor identities.[127]

It is believed that donations to the Clintons were almost certainly being made while Hillary Clinton was serving as Secretary of State, and almost certainly with the intent to influence her decisions. If this is the case, then over the past several years, the Clinton Foundation was basically a foreign money-laundering operation. Foreign nationals could basically pay a foreign charity

---

126 (Davis, 2015)

127 Ibid

— 63 —

designated by the Clintons which then bundled the donations and sent them to the Clinton Foundation. The Foundation then states that it cannot release the names of the donors to their foreign donor and in return the donors receive some sort of political advantages from the Clintons.[128]

It was reported in The Federalist that the Clinton Foundation spun off the bulk of its charitable medical activities in 2010. "By 2013, the main Clinton Foundation entity — the Bill, Hillary, and Chelsea Clinton Foundation — housed only a handful of charitable initiatives, the largest of which existed solely to serve the Clintons, via their conference series and the Clinton presidential library, rather than truly charitable causes. In 2013, for example, the Clinton Foundation spent less than 10 percent of its budget on charitable grants."[129]

The Clinton Foundation is the ultimate fundraising, er... money laundering scheme. Although his name is obviously the organization's name, President Clinton never actually served on its board while Hillary was Secretary of State. What former President Clinton did to retain control of the organization was place Bruce Lindsey on CGEPartnership's board. Lindsey is a long-time Clinton confidant and adviser who also currently serves as the chairman of the board of the Clinton Foundation and is former CEO of the Clinton Foundation for over a decade.[130]

Former Secretary of State Hillary Clinton was not on the board of CGEPartnership, and she was not named to the board of the Clinton Foundation until 2013. Because of this she probably believed that she could claim arm's length from the Foundation and plausibly deny any knowledge of the millions in foreign cash that were being funneled into her family's non-profit coffers.[131]

> If you look holistically at the entire scheme's setup, at the massive flow of foreign cash, at the refusal to disclose donors, at the secret (and now destroyed) private e-mail servers, at the blatantly bogus excuses, at the falsified tax returns, everything about it suddenly makes a lot

128 Ibid
129 Ibid
130 Ibid
131 Ibid

IN GOD WE TRUST

more sense. From soup to nuts, the entire operation was constructed in order to provide a facade of plausible deniability for Hillary Clinton. Conceal the cash. Hide the donors. Delete the e-mails. The circumstantial evidence is overwhelming. In its current form, the Clinton Foundation is a charity in the same way La Cosa Nostra was an Italian soup kitchen. There's a reason a top Clinton executive said of the foundation, "This is not charity. It's a commercial proposition." And that reason is that it's not charity. The simple commercial proposition underlying the Clinton Foundation is access to and potential favors from one of the most powerful couples in the world.[132]

THE SCHIFF SHOW

No one exemplifies the modern-day politician like Democrat US Representative from California, Adam Schiff. This slender gentleman with a very small frame is nothing short of disgusting due to his habitual lying about almost everything.

After the 2016 election, the House of Representatives was one of many institutions that investigated the Trump – Russia farce. This tall tale that the Trump campaign and the President worked with Russia to steal the election away from Hillary Clinton started before the election.

Hillary Clinton mentioned in the third of the three debates with the President-to-be, that Russians may be working with the Trump campaign to rig the election. She even claimed that Republican Donald Trump was a "puppet" for Russian President Vladimir Putin". This was the first this had been said and to most Trump supporters came as a total lie from a woman who was involved in some very corrupt actions herself. It was shrugged off by most of the media but was soon to be revived.

Shortly after the election took place and after the Hillary team waited for recounts in Pennsylvania, Michigan and Wisconsin to take place, the Russia story took off. It was as if the recounts didn't work so let's try this.

The MSM began spinning the story that indeed the President-elect was the puppet of Putin. Again, Trump supporters shrugged it off as evidence that

---

132 Ibid

the Democrats would not accept the election results and were reaching for an excuse.

The problem with the Trump – Russia Hoax was that the media was all on board. They hated the idea of a President Donald J. Trump and were calling for his impeachment before he was even elected. Trump was a brash New Yorker who was in touch with the sentiment of the day – that the media and Washington were corrupt, and the politicians were working harder at padding their pockets than working for the American people. Trump also was not your typical Republican who would sit back and allow the media or his opponents to slander him. He fought back and the media and Democrats hated him for this. Trump was not the apologizing type.

By the time of his inauguration, the Trump – Russia Hoax was in full throttle as leaks of an unsubstantiated and known garbage dossier were selectively reported in the media. Although it was later proven that the dossier was garbage in late 2019 per the report from the Inspector General of the Department of Justice (DOJ IG) on FISA Abuse, the media and Democrats in Congress in early 2017 focused on the dossier as if it was a factual document. No one was more vocal about the Trump – Russia Hoax than Representative Adam Schiff.

Days went on and the Deep State members of Congress, the FBI, DOJ, CIA, State Department and others began investigations culminating with the Mueller investigation. The foxes were in the hen house.

The House Permanent Select Committee on Intelligence was one of the entities that started an investigation into the Trump – Russia Hoax. In 2017, this Committee was led by Republican Devin Nunes. The Democrats' top spokesman was Adam Schiff. This Committee held numerous meetings and brought in a number of individuals close to the Trump campaign and Administration and even members of his family. It seemed that whenever there was a break during the meeting, the media would promote headlines leaked from the Committee meeting that were always detrimental to the Trump team. It was highly suspected that the individual sharing the leaks, which later were proven false, was Adam Schiff.

After nearly a year of looking into the Trump – Russia Hoax, the Republicans were ready to release a document with their findings. So was the

minority, led by Adam Schiff, which decided to release their own report as well. As it turned out the two reports were polar opposites. The Republican report stated that the President did nothing wrong while the Democrat report claimed he was tied to Russia.

More than two years passed and eventually a report was released by the DOJ IG.[133] The report covering FISA abuse addressed the points made by both Nunes and Schiff - the truth was finally out.

Mollie Hemmingway from the Federalist reported the truth based on DOJ IG, Michael Horowitz's report:[134]

> The new inspector general report on FISA abuse settles the debate between Republicans and Democrats on the House Permanent Select Committee on Intelligence. Both groups put out memos about the Department of Justice's efforts to secure a warrant to wiretap Carter Page.
>
> At the time of their release, the media praised Democrat Adam Schiff and his memo and vilified Republican Devin Nunes and his memo. Nearly two years later, the inspector general's report vindicates the Nunes memo while showing that the Schiff memo was riddled with lies and false statements.
>
> The memo from the Republicans on the House Intelligence Committee reported:
>
> 1. A salacious and unverified dossier formed an essential part of the application to secure a warrant against a Trump campaign affiliate named Carter Page. This application failed to reveal that the dossier was bought and paid for by Hillary Clinton and the Democratic National Committee.
> 2. The application cited a Yahoo News article extensively. The story did not corroborate the dossier, and the FBI wrongly claimed

---

133 (Justice, 2019)
134 (Hemingway, 2019)

Christopher Steele, the author of the dossier, was not a source for the story.

3. Nellie Ohr, the wife of a high-ranking Justice Department official, also worked on behalf of the Clinton campaign effort. Her husband Bruce Ohr funneled her research into the Department of Justice. Although he admitted that Steele "was desperate that Donald Trump not get elected and was passionate about him not being president," this and the Ohrs' relationship with the Clinton campaign was concealed from the secret court that grants surveillance warrants.

4. The dossier was "only minimally corroborated" and unverified, according to FBI officials.

All of these things were found to be true by the Inspector General Michael Horowitz in his December 9 [2019] report. In fact, Horowitz detailed rampant abuse that went far beyond these four items.

The Democratic minority on the committee, then led by Rep. Adam Schiff, put out a response memo with competing claims:

1. FBI and DOJ officials did not omit material information from the FISA warrant.

2. The DOJ "made only narrow use of information from Steele's sources about Page's specific activities in 2016."

3. In subsequent FISA renewals, DOJ provided additional information that corroborated Steele's reporting.

4. The Page FISA warrant allowed the FBI to collect "valuable intelligence."

5. "Far from 'omitting' material facts about Steele, as the Majority claims, DOJ repeatedly informed the Court about Steele's background, credibility, and potential bias."

6. The FBI conducted a "rigorous process" to vet Steele's allegations, and the Page FISA application explained the FBI's reasonable basis for finding Steele credible.

IN GOD WE TRUST

7. Steele's prior reporting was used in "criminal proceedings."
8. Each of these claims were found by Horowitz to be false.

Horowitz found that FBI and DOJ officials did in fact omit critical material information from the FISA warrant, including several items exculpatory to Page. Material facts were not just omitted but willfully hidden through doctoring of evidence.

The warrants were based on Steele's dossier, which was known by January 2017 to be ridiculously uncorroborated. The renewals did not find information that corroborated Steele's reporting. The warrants clearly didn't allow the FBI to collect valuable intelligence. And Steele's prior reporting was not used in criminal proceedings.

But this wasn't the end for Schiff. The Democrats in California re-elected Schiff in 2018 and he was actually promoted to the Head of the House Permanent Select Committee on Intelligence, replacing Nunes after the Democrats won back the House. The Mueller report was drafted in early 2018 and next Mueller testified in front of Congress. The presentation by Mueller was less than impressive as it appeared Mueller couldn't qualify as a greeter at Walmart, let along the leader of a Special Counsel investigation of the President. But this didn't stop Democrats and Schiff.

Within weeks the media was abuzz with another fake scandal involving the Trump Administration. Again, Mr. Schiff was right in the middle of it. This time the Democrats and their media moved slightly east, and instead of a Russian scandal, this one related to the Ukraine.

News quickly spread based on more leaked classified information that the President made a call with the new President of the Ukraine where President Trump reportedly withheld aid in a quid-pro-quo arrangement with the Ukraine where he demanded the Ukraine look into the actions of Obama's Vice President Joe Biden and his son Hunter. The media called this situation criminal, even though no such crime is listed anywhere in the US Statutory code.

What the media inadvertently did do was single out Hunter Biden for his actions in the Ukraine while his father was Vice President. Hunter who had

a cocaine addiction was released by the military for this addiction when the largest oil and gas company in the Ukraine hired the young Biden to its Board. Later, Vice President Biden bragged on a video circulated throughout the Internet about how he had a Ukrainian prosecutor fired who was looking into the firm Burisma, where Hunter was on the Board.

In President Trump's call with the new Ukrainian President, President Trump noted that this might be something that the new President might want to look into after President Zelinsky brought it up. Before this, the President asked the young President to look into a firm by the name of Crowdstrike which was owned by a Ukrainian which also was the only firm that confirmed that Hillary's emails were stolen and hacked by the Russians in 2016. It was widely reported that the Russians had hacked the DNC, but the only proof came from Crowdstrike. The FBI relied on Crowdstrike and never checked the server themselves. This incident led to the Mueller Investigation and years of Presidential abuse related to the Trump – Russia hoax.

To put an end to the MSM madness related to the Ukraine scandal and their quid-pro-quo obsession, President Trump released the official transcript from his call with Ukrainian President Zelinsky. The President's actions were perfectly normal, and no quid-pro-quo or criminal activity took place. But this didn't stop the Democrats, the media and the Deep State players involved in this scandal.

The Democrats moved forward and held a public hearing where it was reported that the President had made the call and had numerous quid-pro-quo requests on the call. The information was based on a whistleblower complaint by an individual who was kept anonymous who based his complaint on second hand information leaked to him from the Intel Community. The whistleblower complaint form was altered days before the complaint to allow for second hand information which was never allowed previously.

The Inspector General of the Intel Community (IC IG) who received the complaint and was suspected of making changes to the complaint form, was a key player at the DOJ in 2016 when the Russia collusion scandal started. The whistleblower was reportedly in the White House during the Obama Administration and worked for Joe Biden in the Ukraine as part of his duties

IN GOD WE TRUST

before the 2016 election. Despite numerous actions that would make the complaint ineligible, the IC IG allowed it to move forward.

The Head of the House Permanent Select Committee on Intelligence, Adam Schiff, moved forward. He claimed that he had never met the whistleblower and didn't know who he was, which turned out to be a lie as members of his staff worked with the whistleblower in the Obama White House.

What occurred next was shocking to even those cognizant of Schiff's unabashed practice of lying. During the first open hearing on the Ukrainian scandal, which was being paraded as the beginnings of an impeachment hearing, Schiff claimed that he was reading the President's conversation with the President of the Ukraine, which had previously been released to the public, but he wasn't. Schiff made up the entire conversation between the two presidents.

Democrats laughed about Schiff's lies to the American people and called it a parody. Schiff phrased the call as if President Trump spoke like a mafia boss. It was all a lie. Republicans were stunned. Kayleigh McEnany, from Trump's 2020 campaign, was outraged and claimed Schiff "literally just made up his own transcript."[135]

Next, Schiff held depositions in the basement of the Capital where only Democrats were allowed to call witnesses and have all of their questions answered. The meetings were classified by Schiff which enabled Schiff and others to selectively leak information to the press that was rebutted in the testimonies but not reported publicly to the American public since it was classified.

Then Representative Schiff, moved the hearings to his committee where only certain individuals interviewed in the basement of the Capital were brought in to testify. The IC IG was never brought before the public and to this day his testimony from the Capital basement is the only testimony that has remained classified. Republican House members claim that this is because this testimony would destroy the Schiff Ukraine sham.

Despite no crimes committed by the President, certainly no high crimes and misdemeanors, no treason and no bribery, the Democrats led by lying Adam Schiff voted to impeach the President. Keeping the status quo, the

---

135 (Silva, 2019)

— 71 —

JOE HOFT

House then selected Schiff to be the one who presented the impeachment case to the Senate.

This is the state of politics in the US today. It is no wonder that Americans are not happy with Congress. Adam Schiff is not the only liar in Congress who works for his caucus and not the American people. Americans have had enough.

One solution in dealing with shady politicians is to throw them in jail. If they commit illegal acts, then **they should be put in jail**. Another solution in addressing the low level of trust that Americans have in politicians and to curtail the money grabbing machines the politicians have built, is to institute term limits. The Office of the President of the United States is mandated to serve at maximum only two four-year terms. However, US Senators, US Representatives and Supreme Court Judges are not constrained by term limits. Senators can run for as many six-year terms as they like. Representatives can run for as many two-year terms as they like. US Supreme Court judges also have no limits to their length of service on the nation's top court.

CONGRESSIONAL AND SUPREME COURT RECORD HOLDERS
Democratic Senator Robert Byrd holds the record as the longest serving Senator in US history. He served from January 3, 1959 till June 28, 2010 for a total of 51 years, 5 months and 26 days, more than a half a century.[136] Senator Byrd, from West Virginia, loved dogs and hyperbole, funneled federal dollars into make-work jobs in his native West Virginia and loathed balanced budgets.

Byrd also was a member of the Ku Klux Klan, the racist hate group. He joined the Klan at the age of 24 in 1944 when he refused to join the military because he was afraid he might have to serve alongside "race mongrels, a throwback to the blackest specimen from the wilds," according to a letter Byrd wrote to Senator Theodore Bilbo at the time. When he died there was little talk from the liberal press about his connection with the 'Klan', and if it was mentioned, it was only in passing. No obituaries of Byrd mentioned his 2001 use of the term "white nigger," an early 20th-century anachronism that Byrd mentioned twice during an interview with Tony Snow.[137]

---

136 (Senate.gov, 2015)
137 (Riggs, 2010)

IN GOD WE TRUST

With more than 59 years of service, the longest serving US House of Representative's member was Democrat John Dingle.[138] Dingle set the record as the longest serving Congressman (either Senator or Representative) when he surpassed fellow Democrat, Senator Byrd, in June 2013. Dingle took over his seat after his father's death in 1955. When his father died a special election was held, and young John Dingle, age 29, was voted in as his replacement. During his career in office, one thing Dingle was accused of was stalling the Clean Air Act to curtail additional expenses and fines to his auto interests. His hometown was the Detroit suburb of Dearborn, which was home to a Ford Motor Company factory that was once the largest in the world.[139]

The US Supreme Court has members that are appointed and not elected officials. The longest serving Justice was William O. Douglas who served for 36 years, seven months, and eight days, from 1939 to 1975.[140] Justice Douglas did not only not set the record for the longest tenure on the court, but he also may have set the record for writing the most books during his tenure, more than 30, and most likely holds the record for most divorces and marriages by a Justice over a 13 year time period (four marriages and three divorces) from 1953 through 1966.[141]

Forty-year-old Douglas was appointed to the Supreme Court in March 1939 by Democratic President Franklin D. Roosevelt (FDR). As is the custom today, Presidents pick individuals to be on the Supreme Court that are of the same mindset that they are. Before being a Justice, Douglas was the Head of the Securities and Exchange Commission from 1937 to 1939. Although gifted and with high hopes, Justice Douglas's decisions were disappointedly written more like rough drafts than final prose with many of these drafted within 20 minutes.[142]

Ironic for a judge at such a high position, Douglas's accounts of his own life were undependable. One judge, conservative Justice John Marshal Harlan, once teased Douglas by asserting that "You've told that story so often, you're

---

138 (House.gov, n.d.)

139 (Pergram, 2014)

140 (Supremecourt.gov, 2010)

141 (Garrow, 2003)

142 Ibid

— 73 —

JOE HOFT

beginning to believe it." This was no doubt related to one of the many falsehoods Douglas was accused of making from his own accounts of his early life. He did not suffer from polio as a child, nor did he live in a tent while an undergraduate at Whitman College in Washington State. Although it is reported on his Arlington National Cemetery tombstone that he was a "Private, U.S. Army," some scholars argue that ten weeks of service in the Students' Army Training Corps at Whitman College in late 1918 did not actually make him an Army Private.[143]

Justice Douglas was known for heavy drinking that went together with his sour disposition and nonstop marital escapades. His children stated that he was cold and even 'scary'. He was said to have been on short list with Harry Truman, to be FDR's Vice President, and supposedly never got over the fact that Truman, and not he, was eventually selected and later became President. A law clerk who worked for Justice Douglas, told the story of Douglas's soon to be third wife, Joan Martin, once hiding in an office closet to avoid Douglas's second wife. The following summer the 64-year-old Douglas divorced his second wife and married 23-year-old Joan. Later Joan complained to a former Douglas clerk that he beat her up all the time. A few years later Douglas dismissed Joan from his life, took up with an old Washington State girlfriend, and then met a 22-year-old Oregon waitress, who became his fourth wife in mid-1966.[144]

(AT THE VERY LEAST) INSTITUTE TERM LIMITS

If the careers of the longest serving Senator, Representative and Supreme Court Justice are not ample enough support for term limits, then what is? These are only three of the many elected and appointed officials who have long outlasted their welcome. One way, and perhaps the best way, to ensure or promote integrity in our politicians and government officials is to have limits to the time they can be in office. We cannot always pick the best candidates, and we cannot always vote them out of office, so term limits will minimize their impact when they outlast their stay.

---

143 Ibid
144 Ibid

IN GOD WE TRUST

The current law in the US mandates that the President can only be elected to two terms. This was instituted in the 1900's after President Franklin Roosevelt ran for four terms. He would have probably ran for more, and the US would have probably stayed in a depression had he continued to win, if not for his death.

The current law states that the President can only be elected to serve for eight years since there are four years in each term. Similar laws should be set up for the US House and Senate. To be consistent with the Presidential limits, US Senators should be limited to two terms or twelve years. US Congressmen and women in the US House should be limited as well, but since their terms are only for two years, perhaps a reasonable limit would be four to six terms or eight to twelve years in office, either consistent with the President or the Senate. The US Supreme Court should also have term limits consistent with the President and Congress.

In his excellent book, *Liberty Amendments*, attorney, author and radio personality Mark Levin recommends term limits for Congress and Supreme Court Justices. Levin provides sound arguments for term limits and proposes limiting service in both the House and Senate to twelve years. Levin argues in his book that limiting time in office was a highly regarded proposal during the Constitutional Congress. He also argued for limiting the service of Supreme Court judges to one twelve year term as well.[145] Because it is so difficult to throw bad politicians and judges out, term limits should be instituted to limit the amount of damage a few bad apples can make on the entire country.

Politicians are like diapers – they're full of it and should be changed often.

America should institute term limits for all elected US Senators, US Representatives and Supreme Court judges consistent with the two-term eight-year limit set for US Presidents. Crooked politicians should go to prison. No one should be above the law, not even Democrats.

---

145 (Levin, 2013, p. Chap 2)

4

TRUTH AND HONESTY FROM OUR GOVERNMENT

THE ELECTION OF President Trump had some interesting results, the oddest being how individuals and entities who were once held in great regard were suddenly outed as frauds and fakes. It was as if a spotlight (and not a halo) suddenly appeared on these individuals and America could see them for what they really were and what they had become during the Obama years. These individuals and entities from both sides of the isle showed their true colors and Americans noticed.

The US government became massive under President Obama. In Obama's first year, the US annual budget increased by $1 trillion. The costs of running the government have never been the same after the annual spend increased from $3 to $4 trillion.

THE FEDERAL RESERVE (THE FED)

Citizen Donald Trump was complaining when the US Federal debt was $16 trillion, but today the federal debt is far worse. The debt is the total amount of money borrowed and owed by the government at a given moment in time. When Obama took over in 2009 the US debt was somewhere near $9.6 trillion.

— 76 —

IN GOD WE TRUST

Obama's administration averaged well over $1 trillion in deficits per year. As of late 2014, the US debt load had reached more than $18 trillion.[146] By the end of Obama's eight years, the amount of US debt stood at $19.9 trillion.

One of the major challenges for the government as the debt grows is the increasing size of interest payments on the debt. The Congressional Budget Office (CBO) in 2014 estimated that the federal government's net interest payments on the federal debt will accelerate over the next decade and more than triple, reaching $808 billion in 2025. The CBO predicted that as the interest payments increase policymakers' will be restricted on their ability to use tax and spending policies to respond to unexpected future challenges, such as economic downturns or financial crises. Eventually the continued growth in the debt could lead investors to doubt the government's willingness or ability to pay its obligations, which would require the government to pay much higher interest rates on its borrowing going forward.[147]

Even more alarming than the amount of the US federal debt and deficits is the ever-increasing amount of the US's unfunded liabilities. Unfunded liabilities are promises made for future benefits where no money has been set aside to pay for these promises. The current US fiscal debt is small when compared to the massive amount of growing US government unfunded liabilities. The actual liabilities of the federal government—including Social Security, Medicare, and federal employees' future retirement benefits—exceeded $86.8 trillion in 2012. These numbers do not appear in any US government balance sheet which is why many Americans have not heard of them. However, they can be found in separate reports of actuarial estimates produced by government entities like Medicare and Social Security. As of April 2012, the net present value of the unfunded liability of Medicare was $42.8 trillion. The comparable liability for Social Security alone was $20.5 trillion.[148] Other more recent estimates are that the amount of US unfunded liabilities is over $200 trillion. According to

---

146 (Chantrill, 2014)

147 (Welsh, 2015)

148 (Archer, 2012)

the CBO the present value of the unfunded liabilities, discounted to early 2014 was $205 trillion.[149]

President Trump inherited a mess when he won the Presidency in November 2016. America was ready for real change after Obama's eight years. Obama's economy-killing actions related to massive regulations that killed jobs in the coal, oil and gas fields and other areas, needed to be lifted. President Trump promised he would do just that and in part, because of this, Trump won the election.

But after keeping the Fed Funds rate at 0% for seven of Obama's eight years in office, the Federal Reserve (The Fed) appeared to do all it could to prevent President Trump from having a better economy than President Obama. The Fed increased the Fed Funds rate by a quarter of a percent in late 2015 for the only increase under Obama's time as President. But before President Trump could even raise his hand at his inaugural, the Fed increased the Fed Funds rate by another quarter percent for the only rate increase in all of 2016.

Despite the rate increase, the economy charged forward. American industry and all of America were excited. The incoming President Trump worked hard to encourage companies to do business in the US by meeting with their leaders in droves. **The markets reacted and the greatest stock market rally in US history ensued.**

President Trump next worked hard to implement major tax decreases and the Fed reacted in an almost possessed manner. As the markets rose, the Fed increased rates**. Eight times over two years after the 2016 election the Fed increased the Fed Funds rate**:[150]

Initially the rate increases were almost ignored by the markets but then they began to take a toll. As the Fed increased rates, the markets began to stall and take time to regroup before again reaching new all-time highs.

The markets reached a new all-time high the day after the 2016 election and never looked back through all of 2017. As noted above, despite the Fed Funds rate increase at the end of 2016 and three rate increases in 2017, the markets in 2017 enjoyed their best year ever!

---

149 Op cit, North.

150 (System T. B., 2020)

IN GOD WE TRUST

2019

Make Full Screen

Date	Increase	Decrease	Level (%)
October 31	0	25	1.50-1.75
September 19	0	25	1.75-2.00
August 1	0	25	2.00-2.25

Back to year navigation

2018

Make Full Screen

Date	Increase	Decrease	Level (%)
December 20	25	0	2.25-2.50
September 27	25	0	2.00-2.25
June 14	25	0	1.75-2.00
March 22	25	0	1.50-1.75

2017

Make Full Screen

Date	Increase	Decrease	Level (%)
December 14	25	0	1.25-1.50
June 15	25	0	1.00-1.25
March 16	25	0	0.75-1.00

Back to year navigation

2016

Make Full Screen

Date	Increase	Decrease	Level (%)
December 15	25	0	0.50-0.75

In early 2018, the markets were on fire. The new tax law and the expectations this would positively have on the economy lit up the markets, so the Fed stepped up its market killing policy of increasing the Fed Funds rate. Despite no inflation concerns at all, in 2018 the Fed increased the Fed Funds rate four times. The Fed's last increase took place while the markets were tanking and down 10% since their prior all-time high. The Fed acted insane or like a group of radical liberals attempting a coup on the government by killing the economy.

— 79 —

Fed Head Jerome Powell and the Fed gave America one hell of a Christmas present at the end of 2018 with markets down 20% from their highs in October 2018. **In addition to killing the markets, Powell and gang had singlehandedly increased the US Debt by $1 trillion and mugged the GDP growth rate to year-lows, preventing the GDP from exceeding 3% for the first time in years.** The higher Fed rates also meant that the US dollar was much higher than US competitors. What a mess.

The Fed finally realizing that any more rate hikes and they would be at risk of a lynching, curtailed its rate hikes. However, by August of 2019 President Trump was so disgusted in Powell he asked in a tweet who was worse for America, China's President Xi or the Fed's Jerome (Jay) Powell?[151]

> As usual the Fed did NOTHING! It is incredible that they can "speak" without knowing or asking what I am doing, which will be announced shortly. We have a very strong dollar and a very weak Fed. I will work "brilliantly" with both, and the U.S. will do great...
>
> ....My only question is, who is our bigger enemy, Jay Powell or Chairman Xi?

The President's tweet was blunt and direct. After costing America billions, the Fed finally began to decrease the Fed Funds rate in August 2019, and by November the markets were again reaching all-time highs.

Jerome Powell and his gang at the Fed have done a terrible job working for Americans in an effort to build and strengthen the US economy. Their mandate is to do just that, and they have failed. They failed so badly that there is more evidence to show that they worked to sabotage the Trump economy than to build and strengthen it.

After a few more rate reductions (three in total in 2019) the US markets are again on the rise. Fed-Head Powell met with President Trump on Monday November 18th and the President tweeted:[152]

---

151 (Trump, @realdonaldtrump, 2019)
152 (Trump, @realdonaldtrump, 2019)

IN GOD WE TRUST

Just finished a very good & cordial meeting at the White House with Jay Powell of the Federal Reserve. Everything was discussed including interest rates, negative interest, low inflation, easing, Dollar strength & its effect on manufacturing, trade with China, E.U. & others, etc.

The interest rates are still too high tweeted the President:[153]

At my meeting with Jay Powell this morning, I protested fact that our Fed Rate is set too high relative to the interest rates of other competitor countries. In fact, our rates should be lower than all others (we are the U.S.). Too strong a Dollar hurting manufacturers & growth!

Powell was so frightened by this meeting with the President being misconstrued by the corrupt media that he immediately issued a statement:[154]

The Fed statement asserted Powell's comments were consistent with last week's congressional testimony and did not concern 'expectations for monetary policy,' except to say it will depend entirely on new economic information.

'Finally, Chair Powell said that he and his colleagues on the Federal Open Market Committee will set monetary policy, as required by law, to support maximum employment and stable prices and will make those decisions based solely on careful, objective and non-political analysis,' the statement said.

Jerome Powell and the Fed are a joke. We know what they are supposed to be doing but it appears that the Fed is doing the opposite!

---

153 (Trump, @realdonaldtrump, 2019)
154 (Caralle, 2019)

— 81 —

JOE HOFT

According to its own website:[155]

> The Federal Reserve System was created on December 23, 1913, when President Woodrow Wilson signed the Federal Reserve Act into law. The system is composed of a central, independent governmental agency--the Board of Governors--in Washington, D.C., and 12 regional Federal Reserve Banks, located in major cities throughout the nation.
>
> Today, the Federal Reserve sets the nation's monetary policy, supervises and regulates banking institutions, maintains the stability of the financial system, and provides financial services to depository institutions, the U.S. government, and foreign official institutions.

The Federal Reserve System is complex, and its activities are important and somewhat ambiguous. But most importantly, the Federal Reserve is powerful. Its actions can and do impact all Americans in either positive or negative ways.

When President Trump took over on January 20, 2017, the US was in a mess in almost every way. The economy and foreign policy were in shambles. The US was facing another recession and a large swath of the Middle East was run by ISIS and Iran. President Trump really had his work cut out for himself.

Little did the President know that at that same time the 'Deep State' was mounting a campaign to overthrow his Presidency and they had been working on this for months. Somehow and miraculously, the President made it through this while addressing the country's most pressing concerns.

But one major challenge for the President was the economy. The President worked diligently to encourage companies to stay in the US and to come to the US and produce their goods at home in the US. Deals were cut with Canada, Mexico, Japan, South Korea and others that would encourage fair trade, not just free trade.

A major move by the President was to lower taxes for Americans and American companies to historically low rates. The President also simplified the tax code. The result was to make the US tax regime nearly as simple as the world's best in Hong Kong.

---

155 (System B. o., 2020)

IN GOD WE TRUST

The President also freed up companies by eliminating burdensome regulations. He got rid of regulations that prevented coal mining and oil drilling. Within a couple of years, the US became an oil producer and the world's number one producer of oil.

The economy was on fire because of the President's hard work and initiatives. Of course, the economy was going to fly, it had to.

The President's actions were so positive that it looked like the US could begin paying off some of its trillions in debt. **President Trump had discovered the way to reduce debt, through a massively expanding economy.** But then the Fed and Jerome Powell stepped in to crush it by raising rates at the pace of madmen. To hell with Americans' 401k's, President Trump must be stopped!

Another problem with the Fed increasing rates, was what all Americans feared, and many dreaded. Increased rates meant increased interest payments on the debt. A one percent increase in the Fed Funds rate would equal a $400 billion increase in interest payments on $20 trillion in debt.

Through the first three years of President Trump's tenure as President the US debt grew from $20 trillion to $23 trillion at the end of 2019. Although the $3 trillion increase in US debt under President Trump was not as bad as the $5 trillion increase in debt incurred in Obama's first three years, it was still $3 trillion. Had the Fed left rates at the zero-interest rate that the Fed provided to Obama, the increase in debt under President Trump would have been at least $1.2 trillion less. The debt could have begun to be paid off had the Fed left the economy alone and allowed the markets and economy to grow without the Fed's illogical and abusive barriers.

Why did America ever give a group of unelected individuals the ability to destroy the economy, reduce American's investments and increase the amount of US Debt?

THE CORRUPT DEEP STATE
Along with the increase in spending during the Obama years came an increase in corruption. But the amount of corruption within

— 83 —

the 'Deep State' was shocking, and as the Trump Presidency transitioned into power the Deep State began to show its evil face.

OBAMA'S HABITUAL SPYING

At Trump rallies before the election people cheered 'Drain the Swamp'. America had no idea how corrupt and deep the swamp was in the US at this time. While Americans were attending Trump rallies, Deep State crooks in the government were designing the future President's demise, a coup of the President-to-be was in the works.

After FBI Director James Comey exonerated Hillary Clinton in a press conference in July 2016, conservatives had enough. How could he do this? Comey listed numerous crimes that Hillary Clinton committed as Obama's Secretary of State related to her emails. Classified documents were not protected, when subpoenaed the Clinton team destroyed evidence multiple times. We later found out that her team was allowed to be in the same room with her when she was interviewed by the FBI. The individuals who ran the investigation drafted Comey's exoneration letter months before even interviewing her.

Regardless, Comey shared the following after listing the battery of crimes Hillary committed and then he let her go:

Although there is evidence of potential violations of the statutes regarding the handling of classified information, our judgment is that no reasonable prosecutor would bring such a case. Prosecutors necessarily weigh a number of factors before bringing charges. There are obvious considerations, like the strength of the evidence, especially regarding intent. Responsible decisions also consider the context of a person's actions, and how similar situations have been handled in the past.

In looking back at our investigations into mishandling or removal of classified information, we cannot find a case that would support bringing criminal charges on these facts. All the cases prosecuted involved some combination of: clearly intentional and willful mishandling of classified information; or vast quantities of materials exposed in such a way as to support an inference of intentional misconduct; or

IN GOD WE TRUST

indications of disloyalty to the United States; or efforts to obstruct justice. We do not see those things here.

To be clear, this is not to suggest that in similar circumstances, a person who engaged in this activity would face no consequences. To the contrary, those individuals are often subject to security or administrative sanctions. But that is not what we are deciding now.[156]

What Comey never shared is that the law doesn't require intent. The fact that Hillary Clinton and her team acted negligently in the creation and handling of her emails while she was Secretary of State was all that was needed per the law. Hillary was guilty, Comey let her go and Americans were very angry.

As if this wasn't enough for the average American who goes to work each week and pays his or her taxes, at the same time that the FBI and DOJ were in the process of investigating Hillary Clinton for her email abuse, they were colluding, spying and setting up members of the Trump team in what was later referred to as the Trump – Russia collusion hoax.

It's still unclear when the Obama Administration first started spying on candidate Donald Trump and his team. Many suspect that Obama was spying on whomever he wanted for most of his Presidency. There were stories of reporters who published non-flattering pieces on Obama who were spied on during his terms in office.

One area where Obama seemed extraordinarily sensitive was regarding his upbringing. This is why he didn't like Arizona Sherriff Joe Arpaio who was outspoken about Obama's past. The Sherriff held a presser in December 2016 where he provided evidence that he claimed showed that Obama's birth certificate was a fake. The Sherriff's deputy outlined their case:

In exacting detail, Zullo explained how a careful analysis of the document's typed letters and words, as well as the angles of the date stamps, proved the forgery.

---

156 (Rhodan, 2016)

— 85 —

JOE HOFT

According to the theory, the birth certificate presented to the public was created after copying and pasting information from the legitimate birth certificate of a woman born in Hawaii. An accompanying video simulated how the text would have been moved.[157]

A short time later, 'Sherriff Joe' was taken to court by Obama's DOJ and eventually charged with a misdemeanor of 'criminal contempt of court' by a Clinton appointed Federal Judge.[158] The Sheriff was not afforded a jury.

Apparently, Obama was not happy with the Sherriff's actions because Obama's DOJ announced they were charging the Sherriff on a misdemeanor charge less than a month before Sherriff Joe's reelection for sheriff of Maricopa County. I've heard the Sherriff speak and he stated that his case was one of the most expensive misdemeanor cases in history. Eventually he was charged, and President Trump later pardoned him.

What Hillary's and Sherriff Joe's cases tell us is that Obama was a very vindictive person and he used his DOJ to target his opponents as well as protect his posse. The way Obama's DOJ targeted Sherriff Joe and protected Hillary Clinton showed that Obama's DOJ was not afraid to expand the law when desired and use the law as a weapon in other scenarios. This became clear in the Trump – Russia collusion sham.

Again, we don't know when Obama first started spying on citizen Donald Trump. It is not out of the question to believe that Obama started spying on him when he claimed Obama's birth certificate was a fraud which would have been before the 2012 election.

We now know that Obama's DOJ and FBI were using the US Intel community data to spy on individuals illegally. This came out in early 2016 in an internal report from the NSA (National Security Agency) Inspector General. This report led to actions by the then Head of the NSA, Admiral Mike Rogers

---

157 (Cassidy, Arpaio: Probe proves Obama birth certificate is 'fake', 2016)
158 (Cassidy, Arpaio found guilty of criminal contempt, 2017)

IN GOD WE TRUST

who instituted changes to the way data was being mined and provided to US Intel Agencies and who then initiated an audit of the entire process.[159]

The results of the audit requested by Admiral Rogers were provided to the FISA Court a few days before the 2016 election and a couple days after the FBI and DOJ made their first FISA warrant request to spy on Carter Page and as a result, candidate Trump.[160]

This is explained in an article on Obama's FISA abuse activities:[161]

The initial warrant [the FISA Warrant on Carter Page], and its three subsequent renewals could have been used to spy on anyone who was in contact with Page, including members of the Trump campaign. **The NSA is allowed to analyze communications "two hops" from its original target. Anyone in direct communication with Page is one hop away, and anyone in communication with those talking to Page is two hops away.**

Based on the above, the Carter Page FISA memo was used not only to spy on Carter Page, the warrant was used to spy on President Trump and everyone who candidate and President Trump had contact with.

The audit report covering the audit Rogers requested was not released to the public until April 2017. It was heavily redacted but what was in the 99-page report was the fact that the government had an institutional 'lack of candor' (i.e. they all lied) and the government was sending mined data on Americans directly to contractors of the American government (the contractor names were redacted). To this day we do not know the individuals whose data was sent to these contractors nor do we know the reason why it was sent.[162]

One individual in the Obama Administration who was in charge of compliance with the FISA program on the part of the government, John Carlin, filed a report to the FISA Court only a month before Admiral Rogers presented his

159 (Carlson, 2018)

160 Ibid

161 (Fakkert, 2018)

162 Ibid

report to the Court. Carlin resigned and his last day was in October 2016. Carlin should have notified the Court when there were indications of wrong doing but there is no evidence that he ever did.[163] Some people to this day believe Carlin was the connection between the DOJ and Obama's White House regarding FISA abuse.

Many conservatives familiar with the actions taken by Obama's Intel Community to spy on candidate and President Trump believe that Admiral Rogers is a very good guy for addressing the issues in Obama's government related to illegally spying on Americans. Rogers also went to Trump Tower after the 2016 election on the morning of November 17, 2016. This was only a week after the election. Admiral Rogers did not tell DNI's Head James Clapper that he was going. It is believed that Rogers told President-elect Trump that he was being spied on because on the evening of November 17, 2016, Trump moved his transition team out of Trump Tower and to Trump National Golf Club in New Jersey.[164]

Obama's Intel Community may have applied for the Carter Page FISA Warrant to provide cover for its previous illegal spying on the Trump team and others during the Obama Administration. Obama's Intel Community may have been trying to provide cover for their illegal spying in the unlikely event that 'Crooked' Hillary Clinton did not win the 2016 election.

Since Carter Page was briefly on the Trump team as a volunteer, the government legitimized spying on candidate and President Trump and everyone Trump contacted as well using the Carter Page FISA Warrant.

FBI lovers Peter Strzok and Lisa Page's text messages were reportedly discovered by the DOJ's Inspector General's team in routine audit activities sometime after the 2016 election. These text messages held much information on what was going on behind the scenes related to the Hillary Clinton email investigation, the investigation that was created in mid-2016 related to President

---

163 Ibid

164 Ibid

IN GOD WE TRUST

Trump's connections with Russia (reportedly labeled Crossfire Hurricane), and the Mueller Special Counsel investigation. Both Strzok and Page were involved in all of these investigations.

One particular text between these two love birds was first redacted when some of the text messages between the two FBI lovers were released by the DOJ. In a later document from the US Senate in June 2018, the same text was unredacted when the Senate released an additional 500 texts to the public. The text that was shared between Strzok and Lisa Page in December 2015 said: "Did you get our oconus lures approved?"[165]

No one really knew what this text was about. 'Oconus lures', what is that? This was until a little know individual on Twitter by the name of Nick Falco (who was soon removed from Twitter for some random and unknown reason) sent out a tweet that claimed that 'oconus' meant outside the US and 'lures' meant multiple spies. If this were true, then the Deep State had multiple spies outside the US that were spying on the Trump team as far back as 2015.[166]

This was shocking because former FBI Director James Comey stated under oath that the Crossfire Hurricane investigation didn't originate until the end of July 2016. The problem with this new information for Comey was that FBI rules prohibit the FBI from spying on an American until a formal investigation was open. [167]

We were the first to report this story and the media immediately pounced on this and claimed that it was a conspiracy theory, especially after President Trump's tweet on the subject.

The day after this story broke, President Trump tweeted:[168]

Wow, Strzok-Page, the incompetent & corrupt FBI lovers, have texts referring to a counter-intelligence operation into the Trump Campaign

---

165 (Hoft J. , Breaking: Senate Releases Unredacted Strzok-Page Texts Showing FBI Initiated MULTIPLE SPIES in Trump Campaign in December 2015, 2018)

166 Ibid

167 Ibid

168 (Trump, @realdonaldtrump, 2018)

— 89 —

JOE HOFT

dating way back to December, 2015. SPYGATE is in full force! Is the Mainstream Media interested yet? Big stuff!

The MSM was interested, but what it reported was that President Trump was promoting a conspiracy theory. ABC News and the entire MSM claimed that the President was out of line promoting a conspiracy with no proof. They also claimed to know how the President obtained the information for his tweet:[169]

> The progression of this particular conspiracy theory – from the depths of Reddit to President Trump's Twitter feed – highlights a recurring tactic Trump has employed since taking office: Embracing an unsubstantiated claim suggested by an outside source, peppering it with innuendo, and tweeting it into the ether for his followers to debate.
>
> This particular incident's genesis appears within the depths of a Reddit thread for conspiracy theories, first appearing on the site on June 4. From there, conservative media outlet Gateway Pundit picked it up.
>
> By Tuesday night, the theory made its way to Fox News' Lou Dobbs. "The word lures – which the FBI originally had redacted – refers to FBI recruited spies," Dobbs said on his show.
>
> Dobbs' guest during the segment, Chris Farrell, Director of Investigations at conservative watchdog Judicial Watch, asserted that the text exchange was evidence of the FBI planting a spy within the Trump campaign.
>
> "It was an intelligence operation directed against then-candidate Trump," Farrell said. "It's indisputable."

ABC News never contacted the Gateway Pundit to ask how we received the information for the post or they would have known that the information came from Faldo. They immediately determined the post was false and the President was promoting conspiracy theories.

---

169 (Bruggeman, 2018)

— 90 —

IN GOD WE TRUST

Wikipedia took up the story as well – not the story that the FBI was spying on candidate Trump back in 2015 – but rather that the President was fooled into tweeting a conspiracy theory on Twitter. To this day and into early 2020, Wikipedia calls the entire 'Spygate' incident or rather the fact that Donald Trump was spied on before the election, a conspiracy theory and it uses the 'oconus lures' incident as proof.[170]

Wikipedia is a good source of information for anything other than politics. When it comes to politics it nearly always reports information with a far-left slant.

Unfortunately for the MSM and Wikipedia, they were wrong, dead wrong. They were so wrong that their efforts to cover this all up, the blatant abuse by Obama's Intel community to spy on Americans and especially the Presidential candidate from the opposing party, Donald J. Trump, looks more like an effort to aid the Deep State in covering up their crimes than in finding the truth.

In December 2019 the DOJ IG released its report on its investigation into the Carter Page FISA warrant applications and there were numerous incidents of the Deep State spying on Americans noted in the report.[171]

We know from Congressional interviews involving Nellie Ohr, the wife of the DOJ's Bruce Ohr, that she was hired by Fusion GPS to obtain dirt on candidate Trump. She started her work in late 2015.[172] So we know that the Deep State was already working on efforts to slander and attack candidate Trump in 2015.

Additional proof of the FBI and/or Intel community spying on Americans came from Sidney Powell. Powell is General Michael Flynn's personal attorney in his case against the government. Powell was hired, replacing Flynn's first attorneys in 2019. Since then Powell has been diligently fighting for Flynn's innocence. Powell represented an individual who was attacked by the Deep State in the early 2000's related to the government's case against Enron and

---

170 (Hoft J. , MUST READ... Evidence Suggests Deep State Asset Joseph Mifsud Was One of the Spies (Oconus Lores) Referred to in Strzok-Page Texts from December 2015, 2019)

171 Op cit, Justice, O.

172 Op cit, Hoft, J MUST READ... Evidence Suggests...

— 91 —

related parties. Powell got to know then FBI Director Robert Mueller and his attorney Andrew Weissmann during this period. She lists their many corrupt acts from this period in her book, *"License to Lie"*.

The same Mueller and Weissmann ran the Mueller investigation on President Trump. Powell knows they are corrupt.

Flynn is one of the individuals suspected of being spied on by Obama's Deep State Intel Community. He was spied on by the government before and after President Trump's inauguration and he has been harassed ever since. Flynn was forced into a guilty plea in late 2017 by the Mueller team after threatening to go after Flynn's son if he didn't agree to the plea. Flynn's attorneys at the time encouraged Flynn to take the deal. Flynn eventually replaced these attorneys with Sidney Powell.

In a filing with the court in September 2019, Powell requested information and interview notes (302's) from the government related to Joseph Mifsud who attended a dinner in late 2015 that General Flynn attended as well. The General was invited by another known spy, Stefan Halper. Up until Powell's request it wasn't known that Mifsud participated in this event as well as Halper. This request by Powell identifies two spies (i.e. oconus lures) who were at the dinner General Flynn attended in late 2015.[173]

Mifsud was noted multiple times in Special Counsel Mueller's report drafted at the end of his investigation into the Trump – Russia farce. Various individuals like James Comey claimed that Mifsud was a Russian spy. Many others believe that Mifsud was a western agent and not a Russian spy because of his connections to the UK and Italian spy services. Mifsud's whereabouts to this day are unknown. He was last reportedly seen in 2017, with some speculation that he may now be dead, but as of early 2020, we really don't know what happened to Mifsud.

THE LEAD UP TO THE MUELLER HOAX

President Trump may have had some indication that he was being set up based on his discussion with Admiral Rogers in Trump Tower in November 2016,

---

173 Ibid

IN GOD WE TRUST

but it is unknown how much he knew. He also may have suspected something based on his intuition or personal sources. But, it is unlikely that the President was aware of the all-out effort by the Deep State, the Democrats and their media to have him removed from the office after he won in the 2016 general election.

In early January 2017 the leaders of the Deep State under the Obama Administration met with President Trump to debrief him on intelligence matters. This meeting occurred the day after some of the same members met with President Obama in the White House. Obama's FBI Director James Comey, who participated in both meetings, stuck around after the meeting with Trump and shared with President-elect Trump the contents of a dossier that Comey claimed was in the hands of the media. President Trump expectedly denied the information presented by Comey and we now know this because after the meeting Comey raced to his FBI laptop and wrote down his notes concerning the meeting.

Comey became the first FBI Director in US history who inserted himself into an investigation of the President of the United States (or any investigation for that matter) by recording his meeting minutes with President-elect Trump. Comey did this numerous times after meeting with President Trump before he was eventually fired by the President.

The meeting in the White House the day before Comey and others met with President-elect Trump, was famously memorialized by the Obama team in a last-minute email on the day of President Trump's Inauguration. Two Republican Senators uncovered this email:[174]

As part of their continued efforts to conduct oversight of the Federal Bureau of Investigation (FBI) and the Department of Justice (DOJ), Chairman of the Senate Judiciary Committee Chuck Grassley (R-Iowa) and Chairman of the Senate Judiciary's Subcommittee on Crime and Terrorism Lindsey Graham (R-South Carolina) discovered a partially unclassified email sent by President Obama's former National Security

---

174 (Grassley, 2018)

Advisor (NSA) Susan Rice to herself on January 20, 2017 – President Trump's inauguration day.

Ambassador Rice appears to have used this email to document a January 5, 2017 Oval Office meeting between President Obama, former FBI Director James Comey and former Deputy Attorney General Sally Yates regarding Russian interference in the 2016 Presidential election. In particular, Ambassador Rice wrote:

"President Obama began the conversation by stressing his continued commitment to ensuring that every aspect of this issue is handled by the Intelligence and law enforcement communities 'by the book'. The President stressed that he is not asking about, initiating or instructing anything from a law enforcement perspective. He reiterated that our law enforcement team needs to proceed as it normally would by the book."

This odd last-minute email written by Rice appears to show an attempt to cover up for President Obama's actions related to spying on the President elect and future President. No President had ever done anything close to what Obama was doing in spying on Trump.

Soon after the meeting between President Trump and the Intel community, the media was reporting all sorts of information regarding the President-elect's and future President's actions with Russia. The dossier presented to the President by Comey was released in the press within days if not hours of the meeting with Comey. The dossier claimed various things, some of which were very nasty, such as citizen Trump was in Russia with hookers.

The media ran this story day and night and the President denied the entire matter. There were daily leaks in the press as the New York Times and Washington Post seemed to have direct access to the Deep State. The press also was very compliant in reporting anything shared with them with no apparent concern for whether the information was true or not. As long as the information besmirched President Trump, the MSM reported it.

The President also had a very difficult time with his incoming team due to the Deep State's actions. He hired General Flynn as his National Security Advisor but his time in the Trump White House was short lived. Flynn was set

IN GOD WE TRUST

up by corrupt agents in the FBI, Peter Strzok and Joe Pientka. These two individuals had been targeting Flynn for some time. They stopped by the White House and didn't tell the General that he was under investigation and didn't afford him an attorney. They returned to the FBI and wrote notes on their discussion with Flynn.

It is believed that the original notes on their discussion with General Flynn stated that he did not lie. Others believe that these notes were edited to indicate that he did lie. The original notes have not been made public or provided to Flynn's legal team to date. The FBI claims the original 302 was lost but others that know the FBI's system for managing records state that this is impossible and that there is an audit trail that would show any edits to the 302 as well as the original 302.

General Flynn was forced to resign after only a few weeks in the Trump White House. He was set up by the Obama holdovers in the FBI and DOJ. Sally Yates was the individual who told the Trump White House that Flynn had lied to the FBI. Shortly after this, Yates was fired by President Trump for insubordination. Three years after the set up in the White House, General Flynn is under a gag order and is in the courts fighting for his innocence after being charged with lying to the FBI.

Losing General Flynn was no doubt devastating to President Trump who had an ally in Flynn. What came next was worse. President Trump picked Alabama Senator Jeff Sessions to be his Attorney General. This was a very important role as Trump campaigned on 'draining the swamp'. However, Sessions turned out to be a disaster. Virtually the day after he was sworn in as Attorney General, Sessions recused himself from everything related to the 2016 election and Russia. What a nightmare this must have been for the incoming President! As the press and Democrats were screaming Russia, Russia, Russia, President Trump's Attorney General decided to recuse himself from the entire matter.

We now know that from his inauguration and into August 2017, the President was targeted and being spied on. The Deep State legitimized their spying through the Carter Page FISA warrant that was based on the garbage dossier paid for by Hillary Clinton that

made all sorts of crude assertions that the FBI knew was fraudulent at the time. This fact came from the DOJ's FISA report on the Carter Page warrants that was finally released more than three years after the Carter Page FISA warrant was put in place.[175]

The DOJ in its report on FISA abuse determined that the FBI relied on one source for the information that was used in the FISA warrant that came from the fraudulent dossier. The FBI spoke with the key source used in the dossier that supported the FISA warrant and he said that all the information in the dossier was basically small talk that took place over some beers. None of it was true. This was known in January 2017 before the inauguration and before the media released the dossier to the public. No one at the FBI or DOJ intervened and spoke out about the fact that the dossier was garbage.[176] **Instead a group of Deep State mobsters running the DOJ and FBI, holdovers from the Obama Administration, moved ahead with their illegal coup.**

The FBI, DOJ and other Deep State players continued in their efforts to remove President Trump from office. Every day reports were pushed in the press about how the President was tied to Russia and how he was being blackmailed as a result. Despite the President's efforts to put his policies and plan in place, which he did, the press only reported on the fake Russia collusion story. None of the President's accomplishments were reported, certainly not to the extent the Trump – Russia collusion hoax was paraded in the press.

Eventually President Trump fired FBI Director Comey. It was long overdue. But the MSM, after having crucified Comey for his presser announcing Hillary's exoneration in July 2016 and then again in late October 2016 for reopening Hillary's email investigation, changed its tune. The press encouraged Comey's attacks of the President in the media and placed Comey in the role of a victim after being fired.

The firing of Comey was used by the Democrats, the Deep State and their media as the reason for the creation of a Special Counsel to investigate

---

175 Op cit, Justice O....

176 Ibid

IN GOD WE TRUST

Trump – Russia collusion. The Mueller Special Counsel was created on May 17, 2017, by Deputy Attorney General Rod Rosenstein.[177]

There were many memorable events that followed but perhaps none as memorable as fired Director Comey's testimony in front of the US Senate on June 8, 2017. Up until this time and even after, the FBI Heads, Comey and Mueller, had demanded respect in front of Congress. Looking back, you can see the many times that they refused to answer questions and perhaps lied under oath. This became clear after the Hillary email debacle and was in full force when Comey landed in front of the Senate on this day in June 2017. But Republican Senators were still unaware of how corrupt Comey was.[178]

I remember watching Comey's presentation in shock. I could not believe the effort that he gave to guarantee President Trump was removed from office. This testimony also showed me that you cannot trust Democrats in the Senate and some Republicans as well. I remember calling my brother Jim from Hong Kong and just shaking my head as we revisited the comments made by Comey in his testimony.

One surprising moment during this testimony was when Comey admitted that he met with Special Counsel Robert Mueller before his testimony. What was that? The surprise was that no one in the Senate pressed Comey about what was said with Mueller and then later never challenged Mueller on his blatant conflicts of interest.

In his testimony Comey gave an effort like non-other. He attempted to be pious and holy, even as he walked in the room. (No wonder the FBI's nickname for Comey was 'Cardinal Comey'). Comey glorified his record. He expressed shock from his firing. He claimed the President slandered the FBI when the President stated that it was a mess as a result of Comey being there.[179]

Comey then went after the President as well as General Flynn. He said there may have been collusion between the Trump team and Russia. Comey was asked about the Steele dossier by Senator Richard Burr. We now know that

---

177 (Johnson, 2017)

178 (Mills, 2017)

179 Ibid

— 97 —

JOE HOFT

the FBI knew back in January 2017 that the dossier was garbage at the time it was leaked to the press:

> **BURR:** …At the time of your departure from the FBI, was the FBI able to confirm any criminal allegations contained in the Steele document?
> **COMEY:** Mr. Chairman, I don't think that's a question I can answer in an open setting because it goes into the details of the investigation.[180]

Comey lied and he did this to ensure the Russia collusion sham stayed open, so the FBI could continue to legitimize spying on President Trump and his team. Later in the interview Comey out of the blue admitted to leaking documents to the press.

Of course, the people who voted for President Trump knew the Mueller investigation and the Trump – Russia collusion claim was a hoax and a farce. **The President's supporters' determination to stand behind the President during the years that followed was what the Deep State never counted on.** The liberal congregation bought the Russia collusion sham, hook, line and sinker. They never imagined the rest of America not following along with the Democrats, their MSM and the Deep State's sham.

CROWDSTRIKE'S CONFIRMATION

Maybe America would have gotten on board with the 'Russia Collusion Delusion' had the Deep State players in the Obama Administration not been so corrupt. But for eight years Americans saw too many incidents where things just didn't add up. Americans were wising up.

In Benghazi, for example, four Americans, including a US Ambassador, were murdered after an all-night raid on US personnel and the Obama Administration said this was caused by a video from a guy in Los Angeles. In the 'Fast and Furious' scandal it looked like the Obama Administration was caught running guns to Mexico when a US border agent was killed by someone

---

180 Ibid

IN GOD WE TRUST

using one of the guns. In the Iran deal, Obama's team gave the Iranians, the world's number one terrorist state, billions of dollars. In the IRS scandal, the IRS was caught targeting conservatives, but nothing happened to the accused. The list went on and on. Hillary's email exoneration was just another brick in Obama's corruption wall. Americans had enough!

When the news came out in the summer of 2016 that Hillary Clinton's emails had been hacked by the Russians, no one listened. It was like the boy crying wolf. How much BS could Americans take?

The Russia collusion farce soon began in full force in the summer of 2016 at the time of the DNC convention. It was reported in mid-June that Russia hacked the DNC in a report at the far-left Washington Post:

> In the wee hours of June 14, the *Washington Post* revealed that "Russian government hackers" had penetrated the computer network of the Democratic National Committee. Foreign spies, the *Post* claimed, had gained access to the DNC's entire database of opposition research on the presumptive Republican nominee, Donald Trump, just weeks before the Republican Convention. Hillary Clinton said the attack was "troubling."
>
> It began ominously. Nearly two months earlier, in April, the Democrats had noticed that something was wrong in their networks. Then, in early May, the DNC called in CrowdStrike, a security firm that specializes in countering advanced network threats. After deploying their tools on the DNC's machines, and after about two hours of work, CrowdStrike found "two sophisticated adversaries" on the Committee's network. The two groups were well-known in the security industry as "APT 28" and "APT 29." APT stands for Advanced Persistent Threat—usually jargon for spies.[181]

This shocking claim was the basis for multiple investigations and a special counsel which cost the country tens of millions of dollars over the next few

---

181 (Rid, 2016)

JOE HOFT

years. (What was never investigated were the numerous crimes and seedy acts committed by Democrats identified in the DNC emails released by WikiLeaks prior to the 2016 election.)

To this day Crowdstrike claims its efforts in identifying Russians hacking the DNC were legitimate:

> CrowdStrike Services Inc., our Incident Response group, was called by the Democratic National Committee (DNC), the formal governing body for the US Democratic Party, to respond to a suspected breach. We deployed our IR team and technology and immediately identified two sophisticated adversaries on the network – COZY BEAR and FANCY BEAR. We've had lots of experience with both of these actors attempting to target our customers in the past and know them well.[182]

This investigation by Crowdstrike was the only investigation performed on the DNC's server. The FBI and no other party were allowed to investigate the DNC's 'hacked' server. FBI Director James Comey testified to this in January of 2017. The DNC claimed that the FBI never asked to see their servers, but Comey told the Senate Intelligence Committee in January 2017 that the FBI did, in fact, issue "multiple requests at different levels" to the DNC to gain direct access to their computer systems and conduct their own forensic analysis.[183]

The fact that the FBI and DOJ didn't investigate the DNC server themselves caused even far-left publications like Slate to wonder:

> So if the FBI didn't ask for access the DNC's servers out of laziness or negligence, it certainly should have. And if the DNC denied them that access for fear of being embarrassed by what they might find, or because they had more faith in CrowdStrike than the FBI, then it served only to undermine confidence in the ultimate results of the

---

182 (Lines, 2020)

183 (Wolff, 2017)

IN GOD WE TRUST

investigation and give the impression of having something shameful to hide. Neither the DNC nor the FBI should have been satisfied with an investigation that did not involve the FBI conducting a firsthand look at the compromised systems. And all of us should be concerned about the seeming acceptance of both parties to let a private company singlehandedly carry out an investigation with such significant political consequences.[184]

Yes, the FBI's inaction in reviewing the DNC server was even suspicious to Slate. Another problem with using Crowdstrike exclusively for the task of investigating the DNC's server was Crowdstrike's connections. Crowdstrike is connected to the Atlantic Council (a far-left group) which has connections to the Ukraine. Crowdstrike's Chief Technology Officer is a nonresident senior fellow in cybersecurity at the Atlantic Council. His name is Dmitri Alperovitch (owner of CrowdStrike). In addition, serving on the International Advisory Board of the Atlantic Council, is Obama's Director of National Intelligence, James Clapper.[185]

The additional problem for the FBI, DNC and Crowdstrike was that any additional information that would prove that the DNC was not hacked or was not hacked by Russia would be devastating. This would destroy their entire story. Unfortunate for them, this is the case.

Bill Binney became infamous for his work with the National Security Agency (NSA) in the 1990's before 9-11. He and his team developed a system that could process information as it was collected from communications worldwide and even chart relationships real-time. He believed his system would have identified the 9-11 terrorists before 9-11. In addition, Binney's system also had the ability to anonymously decipher information preventing unlawful breaches

---

184 Ibid

185 (Hoft J. , MAJOR FIND: More Ammunition for Roger Stone: The Only Firm to Review DNC Server, Crowdstrike, is Connected to James Clapper, The Atlantic Council and More Shoddy IT Investigative Work, 2019)

JOE HOFT

to privacy.[186] Binney is 'A Good American' as is told in a documentary by the same name currently available on YouTube.

Binney announced in mid-2019 that per his investigation of the DNC emails released by WikiLeaks in 2016, the emails were not hacked. He added the following:

"The problem with the Mueller report and the Rosenstein indictment is it's all based on lies. I mean the fact they're still lying about the, saying the DNC was hacked by the Russians and the Russians gave it to WikiLeaks.

Well, we had some of our people and our group, the VIPS, the Veteran Intelligence Professionals, look at the data that WikiLeaks posted on the DNC data. They actually posted the DNC data...

...that entire set of data was read to a thumb drive or a CD Rom then physically transported. Now this is what Kim Dotcom is saying. This is what Julian Assange basically was inferring. Others have been saying the same things."[187]

Binney and his team of experts were able to determine that the emails published by WikiLeaks online were not hacked. The speed with which the emails were copied was the key and the emails could never have been hacked and copied over the Internet at the speed in which they were copied. They could have only been copied to a flashdrive or similar device.

If this is the case, then who copied the emails? Some people believe that it may be and individual by the name of Seth Rich. This theory was immediately declared a conspiracy theory by the MSM (which indicates there may actually be something to it).

Rich was a young staffer in the DNC in 2016 who also happened to like Bernie Sanders. It is believed that he was disgruntled with what he saw occurring

186 (Mayer, 2011)

187 (Hoft J. , Esteemed NSA Whistleblower Bill Binney Says He Has Evidence DNC was NOT Hacked – "The Mueller Report and the Rosenstein Indictment Is All Based on Lies!", 2019)

IN GOD WE TRUST

at the DNC in its efforts to prevent Sanders from winning the Democrat candidacy for President over Hillary Clinton. It is posited that sometime in 2016 Rich copied emails onto a flash drive which were then provided to WikiLeaks. To this day, Julian Assange the founder of WikiLeaks claims that no state entity provided the DNC emails to WikiLeaks before the 2016 election and he says he can prove it.[188]

Early one morning in Washington, D.C., young Seth Rich was gunned down. He was shot in the back. The police were on the scene quickly and initially thought that Rich was going to live. Their body cameras have mysteriously since disappeared. Rich was carted to the hospital, but he died a few hours later. The police wrote up the crime as a botched burglary but Rich's wallet, credit cards, watch and phone were not taken. In his honor, the DNC put up a bike rack in his name at its DC headquarters.[189]

At the time of Rich's murder, Donna Brazile was the Interim Chair of the DNC. Brazile wrote a book after the 2016 election which she dedicated, in part, to Seth Rich. She wrote that she was haunted by the death of Seth Rich and was so paranoid of snipers taking her out that she closed her blinds at night after his death.[190]

We don't really know all the reasons why Brazile was so scared of snipers after Rich's murder, but it does seem a bit over the top after her work colleague was murdered in a 'burglary'. Maybe it had something to do with a comment in one of the thousands of emails from Hillary Clinton's Campaign Manager, John Podesta, that were released by WikiLeaks in the fall of 2016. Podesta wrote, "'I'm definitely for making an example of a suspected leaker whether or not we have any real basis for it."[191]

The Seth Rich saga is still ongoing. Attorney Ty Clevenger represents a client who claims that he had information that Rich was the individual who provided WikiLeaks the DNC emails. In one document Clevenger received related to his case, the FBI suggests that the Obama White House pushed intelligence

---

188 (Sundance, 2019)

189 (Powe, 2018)

190 (Caplan, 2017)

191 (Lalia, 2017)

agencies to publicly blame the Russians for email leaks from the Democratic National Committee to Wikileaks. Clevenger wrote in a post referring to his case:

> This afternoon I received an undated (and heavily redacted) transcript of an interview of James Rybicki, former chief of staff to former FBI Director James Comey, that includes this excerpt: "So we understand that at some point in October of 2016, there was, I guess, a desire by the White House to make some kind of statement about Russia's..." and then the next page is omitted.[192]

In 2019 Clevenger filed a FOIA request on any information the FBI might have on Seth Rich. Clevenger fought for months with the FBI, going back and forth to no avail. The FBI claimed there simply was no information in their records related to Seth Rich. Then in early 2020, an FOIA request by Judicial Watch turned up numerous emails between dirty cops Peter Strzok and Lisa Page with the header, 'Seth Rich'. The FBI was caught again withholding evidence in this case that is still ongoing.[193]

Whether you believe Seth Rich provided emails to WikiLeaks or not, there must be something questionable in Crowdstrike's confirmation that Russia hacked the DNC's emails because this was the 'favor' asked by President Trump in his infamous call with the newly elected President of the Ukraine in the summer of 2019.

The Democrats obtained leaked information of the call and used this to impeach President Trump right before Christmas in 2019. The Democrats really had no case they just wanted to impeach Trump. There were no crimes in the Democrats' impeachment sham only accusations that President Trump asked President Zelinsky to investigate the Bidens for their corrupt acts in the Ukraine that occurred during the Obama Administration. Conservatives argue that President Trump had a duty to address corruption on the call with

---

192 (Hoft J. , BREAKING EXCLUSIVE: FBI Covered Up Strzok and Page Emails Regarding Seth Rich – Now the FBI Is Doubling Down In their Cover-Up, 2020)
193 Ibid

IN GOD WE TRUST

the Ukraine. But what many people don't realize is that the favor initially asked of President Zelinsky related to Crowdstrike, not the Bidens.

Per the transcript of the call (that showed that the President did nothing wrong), the President asked about Crowdstrike:

> I would like you to do us a favor though because our country has been through a lot and Ukraine knows a lot about it. I would like you to find out what happened with this whole situation with Ukraine, they say Crowdstrike... I guess you have one of your wealthy people... The server, they say Ukraine has it. There are a lot of things that went on, the whole situation. I think you're surrounding yourself with some of the same people. I would like to have the Attorney General call you or your people and I would like you to get to the bottom of it. As you saw yesterday the whole nonsense ended with a very poor performance by a man named Robert Mueller, an incompetent performance but they say a lot of it started with Ukraine. Whatever you can do, it's very important that you do it if that's possible.[194]

As much as the Democrats, their MSM and the Deep State claimed President Trump was after the Bidens, the real target for the President was Crowdstrike, the Bidens just happened to be identified by President Zelinsky as being corrupt as well!

MUELLER'S NEXT STEPS

Special Counsel and former FBI Director Robert Mueller had to know the day that he was appointed in May 2017 that there was no Russia collusion between President Trump and his team and Russia. We know this because as noted above, it was stated in the DOJ IG report released in December 2019 that the FBI knew in January 2017 that the Steele dossier was total garbage and this was the essential part of the FISA warrant application obtained on Carter Page to spy on the

---

194 (Dunleavy, 2019)

Trump team. However, no one but the FBI, the DOJ and other US government Deep State actors knew this at the time of President Trump's inauguration.

The narrative in the 'fake news' MSM at the time Mueller's investigation originated that led to the Special Counsel being created was that President Trump's team was tied to Russia and used these ties to swing the 2016 US election towards a Trump win. This again was more absolute BS from the Democrats, their media and their Deep State crooks. Everyone who voted for Trump knew it.

The Mueller gang realized coming in that they needed to create some sort of relationship with President Trump and his team to the 2016 election and Russia. So, they created a made-up story line that would be comical if not so corrupt that continued the most egregious abuse of power in US history.

In early 2019 President Trump's replacement for Jeff Sessions, Attorney General Bill Barr, stepped in and ended the Mueller investigation. Barr must have asked Mueller on his first day what information he had on collusion with Russia and Mueller must have said nothing. Hearing this Barr must have told him to shut it down. Barr probably already knew this because we know now that Mueller likely knew this on the first day of his appointment, if not sooner, that the Russia collusion hoax was a sham.

By the end of his corrupt Special Counsel, Mueller had indicted 38 individuals and three companies. What was most astonishing was that more than three out of four individuals indicted were Russians.

Here is the list of indictments [*which comes in large part from a post of ours published in March 2019*]:[195]

One Lonely Russian Woman Accountant indicted in October 2018 - DAG Rod Rosenstein announced that the Mueller team was indicting a female accountant in Russia for creating more than 400 posts on Facebook that the DOJ says were inflammatory. Nobody saw the posts but that's beside the point. [The timing on this was suspicious because it was recorded in early

---

195 (Hoft J. , After 675 Days of Witch Hunt: More Than 80% of Mueller Indictments Were of Russian Actors Who Will Never See US Courtroom, 2019)

September, but Rosenstein waited until a few days before the 2018 mid-term elections to announce the indictment. This was no doubt an effort to influence the mid-term election against President Trump.]

7 Russian Intelligence Officers (3 previously charged in July) - In early October 2018 the DOJ on behalf of the Mueller team announced that they charged seven Russian GRU officers with crimes. As we noted at the time, the officers will likely never be tried in the United States and three of the men were already charged back in July in connection to the Mueller witch hunt.

12 Russian Intelligence Officers - The Justice Department on July 13 announced that 12 Russian intelligence officers were indicted for allegedly hacking the Democratic National Committee, the Democratic Congressional Campaign Committee and Hillary Clinton's campaign during the 2016 election. All 12 are members of GRU, the Russian intelligence agency.

The indictments, which stem from the Special Counsel Robert Mueller's probe into Russia's efforts to interfere in the 2016 presidential election, were announced by Deputy Attorney General Rod Rosenstein.

Again, we noted at the time, these 12 individuals will never be prosecuted. We really have no information that they did anything to disrupt the 2016 election. The FBI and DOJ cannot be trusted in anything related to the Mueller investigation, so it is not a stretch to believe these indictments are made up like the other Russians indicted. The only thing is with this indictment the individuals indicted may be real people, but who really knows if they had anything to do with our 2016 election.

13 Russians 'Made Up' by the Mueller Team - In an effort to tie their corrupt investigation to Russia, the Mueller team indicted 13 Russians after presenting their cases to a grand jury in February of 2018. Immediately, these indictments were suspect as everyone on the corrupt Mueller team knew that these 'Russians' would never be brought to justice, even if they were real, because they would never come to the US to stand trial and risk being put in jail.

JOE HOFT

General Mike Flynn - The biggest indictment by the dirty cops and attorneys on the Mueller team was the indictment of General Flynn for lying to the FBI. One of the two individuals that Flynn apparently lied to was Peter Strzok in a discussion at the White House shortly after the inauguration. Strzok was the lead investigator who took Hillary Clinton's testimony in her email scandal and was apparently fine when Hillary destroyed her server, 30,000 emails, numerous phones with hammers and lied to him and all of America. Shortly after Flynn spoke with Strzok, former Attorney General Sally Yates from the Obama Administration went to the White House and told the new President the General had lied.

Flynn was fired by the President and then when Mueller started his witch hunt he charged Flynn for lying to the FBI. Flynn eventually pleaded guilty but the judge overseeing his plea was recused. We later found out that the recused Judge, Rudolph Contreras was also a FISA Court judge and a friend of Strzok's.

To date Flynn has not been sentenced and in early 2020 Flynn took back his plea and claims his innocence. Flynn was set up as early as January 2015 and again in the Trump White House in early 2017. Strzok, Yates and McCabe have all been fired.

Paul Manafort - Paul Manafort was President Trump's campaign manager for a short time during the 2016 election. The Mueller team initially charged him with multiple counts of not filling in forms required by the law starting in 2005. In an effort to pay his legal fees, Manafort borrowed money using personal collateral or real estate. Mueller and his team then charged Manafort with bank fraud claiming these loans overstated the value of his properties. Mueller's team then charged Manafort with trying to tamper with witnesses.

Manafort's attorneys argued that the entire case was unconstitutional based on the fact that no crime was committed by Trump which is required to set up a Special Counsel. However, the judge on one of Manafort's cases was Obama appointed Judge Amy Jackson. With her record Manafort would never receive a fair trial as she disagreed with these arguments from Manafort's legal team from the start.

— 108 —

IN GOD WE TRUST

Judge Jackson placed a gag order on Manafort per the Mueller team's request. Soon after Judge Jackson placed Manafort in prison and then in solitary confinement. Today Manafort sits in prison after being indicted on numerous counts.

Besides putting Manafort in solitary confinement, there were other questionable moves by the Mueller gang. For starters, the crimes identified by Mueller were reviewed years before by the FBI which determined that no indictment was required. It was as if the FBI decided to hold on to the information until the opportune time to bring it forward.

Another more questionable action taken by the Mueller team was the fact that Mueller overlooked the Podesta brothers' actions with Manafort. As noted above, John Podesta was Hillary's Campaign Manager whose emails were leaked by WikiLeaks. The Podesta brothers worked alongside Manafort in the Ukraine and brought in a number of US politicians and government officials for photo ops with then Ukrainian President Poroshenko. Included in these events were Hillary Clinton and even Mueller himself. We don't know how much these individuals were paid for their pics with the Ukrainian President. In the end, Mueller gave Tony Podesta immunity for testifying against Manafort.[196]

Rick Gates – Richard Gates pleaded not guilty to all charges against him by Mueller, many related to years before the 2016 election. Gates was named alongside Manafort in the charges brought by the special counsel. He was accused of 11 counts related to filing false income tax returns and three counts of failure to report foreign bank and financial accounts.

Gates pleaded guilty and in the wake of the guilty plea, Mueller moved to drop the 22 bank and tax fraud charges against him. Gates eventually worked with the Mueller team to indict his former partner Manafort whom he admitted to stealing from during their time together.

---

196 (Hoft J. , NEVER FORGET: Dirty Cop Mueller Gave Tony Podesta Immunity to Testify Against Manafort After Committing Same Exact Crime, 2018)

George Papadopoulos - Papadopoulos was a young Trump volunteer who traveled to the UK and was set up by spies inserted into the Trump campaign by the FBI in early 2016.

A former foreign policy adviser to Trump's presidential campaign, George Papadopoulos pleaded guilty in 2017 to making false statements to the FBI regarding "the timing, extent and nature of his relationships and interactions with certain foreign nationals whom he understood to have close connections with senior Russian government officials," according to court documents.

Papadopoulos, like the others indicted, was under gag orders until he was sentenced to 14 days in jail. He now is vocal in noting that he was spied on during the 2016 election.

Alex van der Zwaan and Richard Pinedo - These are two individuals no one really ever heard of nor will ever remember. Alex van der Zwan was charged with lying to the FBI. Richard Pinedo was charged for selling bank accounts to Russians, even though Pinedo said he didn't know he was selling accounts to Russians. (Pinedo's case appears similar to the case Obama conjured up in 2011 when an innocent man in Los Angeles was charged with creating a video that led to Benghazi.) Both cases sound suspect and more related to abuse of power by the Mueller team than actual crimes being committed.

Michael Cohen - The Mueller team raided the President's attorney's office, home and storage unit and took all the documents they could – to hell with attorney client privilege. This information then led to Michael Cohen, the President's former personal attorney to plead guilty to some more bogus charges created by the Mueller team. He was eventually convicted of some bogus charges and is now sitting in prison.

Roger Stone – We knew Stone was going to be imprisoned when it was announced that Judge Amy Berman Jackson was assigned to his case. It's unknown how Judge Jackson could be assigned to both Stone's and Manafort's cases.

Stone was charged with lying to Congress, a charge that in today's DOJ, only conservatives qualify. His real crime was being a friend of President

IN GOD WE TRUST

Trump. Stone attempted to have the issue of whether the Russians hacked the DNC addressed in his case because he was being charged for activities related to this. When asked to provide support the FBI provided a redacted document from Crowdstrike which it turned out the FBI never asked to be unredacted.[197] Eventually Judge Jackson ruled against this argument being covered in the case and Stone was found guilty of seven counts and is now facing the remainder of his life spent in prison.

In summary, the Mueller gang indicted 38 individuals, most (Russians) will never see a court room and we really don't know if they are real people or not. The remaining indictments relate to some unfortunate individuals who happened to know Donald Trump.

CONCORD MANAGEMENT'S GRAPES OF WRATH

The Mueller gang thought they were so smart in their actions harassing the newly elected President and the American people, but they really weren't. They thought that because the MSM repeated whatever they wanted made them even smarter. With no challenges from the fourth estate they got cocky. Maybe this led the Mueller team into thinking they were smarter than everyone else. Overall it was a horrible time in US history. (Despite all of Mueller's corrupt acts, the President kept rolling on with his agenda and the US economy and so many other problems left over from the Obama Administration were addressed.)

The one big mistake that the Mueller team made during this time, was trying to tie Russia to the Trump team. The Mueller team did this in at least, three ways. The first way, as noted above, was to indict Russians on efforts that were supposedly criminal that were impossible to prove. The second way was to tie Russia to social media before the election. The third way will be discussed below when Mueller tied three Russian companies to the collusion hoax)

---

197 (Laila, 2019)

JOE HOFT

Mueller's team argued in their final report that Russia had impacted the 2016 election. Far left Russian collusion promoters CNBC posted an article titled: *'Mueller report details how Russians reached millions of US Facebook and Twitter users and brought them out to real-life rallies'*. In the report CNBC shares:

Special counsel Robert Mueller's report released Thursday says Russia's Internet Research Agency, or IRA, reached millions of U.S. users on Twitter, Facebook and Instagram leading up to the 2016 presidential election. Russian operatives also communicated with the Trump campaign under false identities "without revealing their Russian association" and interacted with prominent pro-Trump activists to arrange political rallies, "confederate" events and even a #KidsforTrump organization, the report says.[198]

But this was all a bad joke. Russia's influence on the election was the heart of the fake investigation, and Mueller tried to tie some Facebook posts to the Russian effort to impact the 2016 election using false statements and make-believe hyperbole of Russians impacting the election through the use of social media.

President Trump's son in law said it all after Mueller's report came out when he shared – the Mueller investigation has been far more damaging to our democracy than the Russian spend on Facebook ads. Kushner said that the Russians spent around $160,000 on Facebook ads during the election. This is nothing when compared to Facebook's revenues and the amount of spend by the Trump campaign during the election on overall ads.[199]

Mueller's team first attempted to use the same data in February 2018. It was a hoax then as well as a year later when included in his final report. For one, the US MSM favored Hillary Clinton and 91% of the media coverage on her opponent Donald Trump was negative. The Russians never had a chance.[200]

---

198 (Fazzini, 2019)

199 (Hoft J. , COMPLETE BS: Jared Kushner Explains How Mueller's Junk Report of Russian Facebook Influence Was Deep State Garbage, 2019)

200 Ibid

— 112 —

IN GOD WE TRUST

Facebook executive Colin Stretch told the US Senate Judiciary Committee in November 2017 that the total number of illegitimate ads paid for by Russia according to Mueller were a drop in the ocean — less than 0.004 percent of all content — or about 1 in 23,000 news feed items.[201]

According to Mueller the Russians planned election rallies for Trump and for Hillary. The Mueller report didn't share that the Trump rallies saw a total of 31 people show up. The anti-Trump rallies had a turnout of 10,100 people.[202]

According to testimony in the Senate, the Russians spent a total of $3,111 during the election in Michigan, Wisconsin and Pennsylvania and all but $54 of that total was spent after the primaries. Again, that's a total of a little more than $3,000 in these key states. Facebook's revenues are in the tens of billions, clearly Russia had no impact on the 2016 election via social media.[203]

The third way that the Mueller team attempted to tie Russia to the 2016 election, was by tying three Russian companies to events before the election. The Mueller gang indicted three Russian companies at the same time they indicted the 13 Russians for tampering in the campaign. Unfortunately for Mueller, this turned into a royal mess. Mueller's team knew that none of the Russians, if they were real, would come to the US for trial. They must have felt that by naming three companies in their indictment that it would look stronger, and they too would never show up in the US. But this backfired when lawyers defending one of three indicted Russian companies, **Concord Management**, showed up in court.[204]

Mueller's team was caught off guard and never expected this. They immediately asked the judge for more time, but the judge denied their pleas noting that they were the ones who indicted the Russian company in the first place.

When the case proceeded, the Concord attorneys noted that one of the three companies indicted by Mueller was not in existence at the time of Mueller's indictment. Concord Catering was a sister company to Concord management and it wasn't even in existence at the time Mueller declared.

---

201 Ibid

202 Ibid

203 Ibid

204 Ibid

Concord's attorneys called this a case of Mueller indicting 'the proverbial 'ham sandwich''.[205]

At a following court appearance, the attorneys representing Concord stated that the corrupt Mueller team's allegations of 13 Russian individuals impacting the 2016 election were "made up" nonsense. The individuals were not even real. Mueller's team attempted to connect them with Concord Management, but Concord had never heard of them.[206]

Concord Management's lawyers revealed that Mueller's team had ignored over 70 discovery requests they had made for information in the case. In response Mueller's team offered to give Concord Management's lawyers a massive amount of social media data from those dangerous trolls who sought to influence the US election and the majority of the data was in Russian.[207]

Mueller's lawyers then admitted that they didn't even have English translations for the Russian social media posts. However, somehow Mueller's lawyers believed Americans were influenced by these Russian language posts?[208]

In a follow up brief to the court on October 23rd, Concord Management's legal team began mocking Mueller:

> Concord has consistently argued that the Indictment charges no crime at all (interference with an election), but to the extent it purports to charge a crime the essential element of willfulness is fatally absent. The Special Counsel's retort has been that he was not required to charge willfulness because he did not charge violations of FECA or FARA. Now, in mind-bending, intergalactic, whiplash fashion, he says for the first time, I did, I charged violations of FECA and FARA.(1) Reminiscent of the old adage, "Give a man enough rope and he will hang himself," the Special Counsel just did so.

---

205 Ibid

206 Ibid

207 Ibid

208 Ibid

(1) Which sounds a lot like "I did, I did, I taw a puddy tat." Tweetie (1948)[209]

The Concord Management case quickly turned into a big joke. The Mueller team should have been ashamed for bringing it to the court and should be charged for making the whole thing up. Unfortunately, most Americans didn't even know about any of this because the MSM never reported it.

The corrupt Mueller Investigation ended in the first half of 2019 as the report was issued and Mueller's team stated that they identified no crimes related to Trump – Russia collusion. The report never mentioned that the support for the entire sham investigation was a dossier that the creators admitted was something made up over a few beers. The dossier was a fraud. So were the lies that led up to the Mueller Special Counsel and the investigation itself.

US Representative Devin Nunes stated that the entire exercise as an obstruction trap. The Deep State crooks who conjured this whole thing up knew there was no Russia Collusion. What they planned was to remove the President on obstruction. The Deep State hoped the President would do something that would enable them to make this claim, but he did not.

Despite the corrupt Mueller gang obtaining documents from President Trump's personal lawyer and throwing attorney – client privilege out the window, the President did nothing. The President and his team provided all documents requested to the Special Counsel. The President allowed his White House attorney to be questioned for hours by Mueller. The President didn't retaliate when those close to him were set up. The President didn't retaliate when his family was brought before the courts and Congress for hours at a time. As a result, Mueller had nothing.

This ordeal, which was really a soft coup, was one of the worst periods in US history behind only the Civil War. Deep State Democrat actors in the government took the law into their own hands and desecrated the US Constitution. This can only be corrected by strict penalties for those who participated in the sham and additional controls put in place to ensure this never happens again.

---

209 Ibid

The US government must put in place stiff penalties for individuals within the government who go outside the mission of their duties and mandates. Government employees, especially those in law enforcement and the Intel Community must be held to a higher bar than average citizens and severe penalties should be handed out for breaches to their call of duty and breaking the law. Current criminals in the government should be prosecuted and sent to prison.

5

CONCLUSION

ON FEBRUARY 16, 2017, barely into his first term in office, President Trump said the following:[210]

"As you know, our administration inherited many problems across government and across the economy," he told the assembled reporters. "To be honest, I inherited a mess. It's a mess. At home and abroad, a mess. Jobs are pouring out of the country; you see what's going on with all of the companies leaving our country, going to Mexico and other places, low pay, low wages, mass instability overseas, no matter where you look. The Middle East is a disaster. North Korea -- we'll take care of it folks. We're going to take care of it all. I just want to let you know, I inherited a mess."

At this point in time it is doubtful that President Trump knew that Deep State DOJ, FBI and other Deep State government holdovers from the Obama Administration were in the process of spying on him in an effort to have him removed from office. It's also unknown why President Obama's team would go to such depths to prevent President Trump from transitioning into power. What were they trying to hide?

---

210 (Jacobson, 2017)

We don't know if had Hillary Clinton won the election, whether the Deep State would have still gone after Donald Trump, his campaign and his family the way they did after the 2016 election. Knowing how vindictive Hillary was during her career, it is likely that she would have put the assets of the entire government into imprisoning and bankrupting Trump and his handsome family. Regardless, the Deep State attempted to do just that anyways.

Americans would have been punished - the gall of voting for someone other than the chosen Hillary Clinton! The middle class would have been fully destroyed. China would have the largest economy in the world.

After three years in office, President Trump must be impeached the far-left corrupt media declares. The Democrats called for it before the 2016 election and even on the day of President Trump's inauguration.

The Mueller investigation didn't work. It did take away more than two years of resources from the President's, the government's and taxpayers' resources. It tore the nation apart. The media and Democrats blamed Trump. In a sense they were right because Trump won the election, but no one deserved what he went through during his first three years.

Who in their right mind who followed the MSM during the 2016 election would have predicted a Trump win – clearly nobody. The reason is the media was toxic and anti-Trump and unfortunately today it's gotten worse.

But Americans are an amazing group of people. The miracle of the 2016 election was that Americans not only wanted change, but they worked to find the truth and they found it in the new media. They then shared this truth with others on social media.

Americans who love Trump, love him for his brashness and courage in standing up to the evil in the media and the evil politicians in DC. Americans wanted a hero and the media and the Democrat's constant attacks have actually made him just that.

One realization that comes from all this, is the difference between conservatives and liberals. The main difference is where they obtain their information. **Liberals still believe what the corrupt media is telling them. Conservatives don't believe a word of it.**

IN GOD WE TRUST

The other epiphany that is clear about the differences between conservatives and liberals, is conservatives know what liberals are being told in the media. It is clear every day as the corrupt media pushes their liberal agenda upon America. But liberals have no idea what the conservatives are reading and seeing. If they did, liberals would no longer be liberals.

This was clear in the studies by Harvard and the Columbia Journalism review in early 2017. When you look at the media outlets that were most read by liberals, none of the conservative sites were on the list. When you look at some of the media outlets read by conservatives you find the list includes some far-left sources like CNN, the New York Times and the Washington Post.

Liberals don't follow conservative sites because they are prevented from knowing what is being said by their gatekeepers in the DNC and the MSM and because the liberal MSM pushes bogus reports of what is being said on conservative sites. Many times these reports are outright lies (e.g. they are all racists).

Conservatives know what is being promoted on liberal sites because it is being pushed down their throats, for one, but also because conservatives can't believe the crazy, dishonest, anti-American, anti-Christian and disgusting posts and stories promoted by the corrupt MSM. Crazy left-wing MSM reports are big news for conservatives. The corrupt media has no idea how its bogus reporting helps conservatives who promote the truth and who can see and point out the antithesis of the truth pushed by the MSM.

Under President Trump, the media had a choice. It could either change and begin to report more honestly and therefore gain back some credibility and respect, or it could continue more of the same. The corrupt media chose to go all-in on their bogus and corrupt reporting. This major blunder is hurting them now and will in the long run. Americans want the truth. The truth sets us free. The liberal MSM will not report the truth. This position is against freedom in the United States and around the world.

The MSM bias has now come very close to destroying our country. As the Deep State crooks involved in Crossfire Hurricane and the Trump – Russia collusion hoax planned their coup, the MSM played along. Instead of challenging the nonsensical and corrupt actions of the Deep State and reports and leaks

— 119 —

from the Deep State FBI and DOJ, they hired the masterminds behind the coup and brought them into their organizations.

Unelected officials in Obama's White House and Justice Departments ran amuck in efforts to have President Trump removed from office after doing all they could to prevent him from winning the Presidency. The Deep State showed its face and it was ugly. Mueller, Weissmann, Strzok, Page, Carlin, Ohr, McCabe, Rosenstein and many others colluded to remove the President from office.

These same players worked in unison with corrupt politicians, mostly Democrats, but many Republicans as well. The face of political dishonesty and corruption ended up being Adam Schiff. This was the individual that the Democrats chose to use to present their impeachment case in front of the US Senate. The case was so dishonest and corrupt, perhaps Schiff was the perfect person to present it.

Americans have totally had enough. There is a silent majority which is enraged by the corrupt actions of the Deep State and their MSM and politicians. Everyone involved in the coup should be severely punished. These corrupt actors put the US through hell these past few years.

No President since Abraham Lincoln endured the amount of terrible press and hate from Democrats that President Trump endured. Like Lincoln, President Trump charged ahead - boy did he.

In 1860, after Lincoln won the Presidential election, the Democrats did all they could to discount Lincoln's win as well. They seceded from the Union before his inauguration and started their own new confederacy. Next, the Civil War began as the Democrats in the South wanted to keep their slaves, their nemesis was the new Republican President whose party was created with a mission of ending slavery in the US.

It was at this perilous time in our nation's history, that the Lincoln Administration realized the importance of recognizing the country's connection with God:

The motto *"In God We Trust"* rose to prominence as both a religious and political device during the Civil War. This was in response to the

IN GOD WE TRUST

war's carnage and horror following the terrible losses in the war's first few months. According to US treasury documents, the genealogy of the motto on our currency can be traced back to an appeal written to Secretary of the Treasury Salmon P. Chase by Rev. Mark R. Watkinson, a Baptist minister from Ridleyville, Pennsylvania. In the letter dated November 13, 1861 Watkinson expressed concern about the absence of any reference to God on the country's currency.[211]

Secretary Chase did add words to the US currency, "In God We Trust" and it first appeared on US currency in 1864. (Years later in 1956, Republican President Dwight Eisenhower signed a law making "In God We Trust" the nations official motto. This law also mandated that the phrase be printed on all US currency.[212])

The Civil War came to an end in April 1865 with the surrender of Lee to Grant at Appomattox. But the Democrats of that day were not unlike the Democrats of today. President Lincoln had only two weeks to relish in the end of the war before he was assassinated at Ford Theater in Washington, D.C.

Very few people know this, but the assassination of Abraham Lincoln was part of a plot to overthrow the US government. The same night Lincoln was shot, other members of his cabinet were attacked as well. The authorities at the time rounded up several suspected participants and eventually four individuals were charged and hanged for their actions in their attempted coup of the US government.[213]

In December of 2019 I posted the following comparing the coup in the 1860's with the coup of the past few years.

---

211 (Apelbaum, 2020)

212 Ibid

213 (Hoft J. , Four Were Hanged In 1865 Democrat Coup Involving Lincoln's Assassination – None from 2016 Democrat Coup to Take Out Trump, 2019)

This is America's second Democrat coup attempt!

The Democrats and their Deep State and corrupt media connived a plan to remove President Trump through the made-up crime that Trump 'colluded' with Russia to win the 2016 election. This was nonsense as this 'crime' isn't even a crime in our statutory books.

The investigation started without any crime being committed and with a scope that allowed Mueller to look at anything, both against the law. The team put together never would have been allowed in a real court of law because they were all Trump haters and former Hillary Clinton allies. The media never addressed this but then again, the media was part of the attempted coup! There are at least ten reasons why the Mueller coup was unconstitutional and illegal.[214]

Mueller remained silent during the coup while his compatriots in the Deep State DOJ and FBI leaked abusive and dishonest stories to their pawns in the media. The media also kept cheering on Mueller and called him a man of integrity. This was clearly not the case for Mueller's past is full of questionable and corrupt actions while cleaning up messes for the Clintons and other allies in the government.[215]

Eventually Mueller indicted the less fortunate and a group of made up Russians with made up crimes.[216] As of October of last year the Mueller team had indicted 38 individuals and 3 companies, with more than three out of four of the indicted individuals related to Russians who may not even be real and probably had nothing to do with our 2016 election.[217]

---

214 (Hoft J. , Joe Hoft and John Schlafly Discuss The Top 10 Reasons the Mueller Investigation Is Unconstitutional (Video), 2018)

215 (Hoft J. , New Documentary of Robert Mueller Starring Attorney Robert Barnes Shows "He's No Patriot!", 2019)

216 (Hoft J. , At Least FIVE TIMES Dirty Cop Mueller and Andrew Weissmann Created Crimes that Resulted in Indictments of Thousands of Innocent Individuals and Companies, 2019)

217 Updated to agree with numbers above

IN GOD WE TRUST

Mueller's gang was asked to investigate Russian collusion but they only looked at the Trump team and those connected to President Trump. Over 100 times the Deep State DOJ, FBI and Mueller gang deviated from standard practice or committed crimes in an effort to exonerate Hillary Clinton from crimes and indict Trump.[218]

Good men like General Mike Flynn and Roger Stone were mere casualties. Like the Union and Confederate soldiers in the Civil War, to hell with life and liberty, move on with the coup and secession from the Union.

Early on it was suspected that the coup was merely an attempt to harass and remove the President while covering up Deep State crimes. Perhaps it was. Regardless, Americans were very angry with Mueller, the media, the Deep State and the Democrat gang who attempted to overthrow the US government.[219]

Over three years the Deep State, Democrats and the MSM culminated their coup with the Mueller report. After interviewing and harassing individuals literally thousands of times, the coup gangsters put together their report. Tens of millions were spent of tax payer's hard-earned money. No doubt matching amounts were paid out of the pocket by the President and those close to him in attorney fees.

There was no collusion. It was all an 'obstruction trap' as Representative Nunes stated. Attorney General Barr rightly reported 'no collusion and no obstruction'. If the gang who worked with Mueller would have had anything remotely close to a crime, they would have reported it, but they did not because they could not.

Today these criminals walk free. There has been no accountability for their actions. They did everything but murder President Trump and most politicians, including Republicans don't seem to care.

Americans care, and Americans want justice. We all know that if we did anything remotely the same as these crooks in the Deep State, we would

---

218 (Hoft J. , THE LIST: More than 100 Times the FBI, DOJ and/or Mueller Gang "Deviated from Standard Practice" or Committed Crimes in Effort to Exonerate Hillary and Indict Trump, 2019)

219 Op cit, Hoft, J, Four Were Hanged…

be in jail for life. Individuals in the Deep State and politicians who helped them in their attempted coup need to be held accountable. It's time for justice.

In addition, the US MSM needs to change or be made irrelevant. This can only be done with protections for freedom of speech. America must act to protect free speech before this country becomes another communist, fascist nation.

Many Americans believe that America was saved by the election of President Trump. It was but perhaps it is only a reprieve. It's time for us to trust God and have faith that hopefully, just hopefully, justice is served, and the media will remain free.

God bless the USA.

APPENDIX I

JIM HOFT STATEMENT FOR THE SUBCOMMITTEE ON THE CONSTITUTION AND CIVIL JUSTICE

September 27, 2018

Good morning.

Thank you, Chairman King and subcommittee members for organizing this important hearing today.

Your colleagues in Congress have provided a lot of airtime recently to prominent CEOs of tech companies who are trying to put me, and others with my politics, out of business. I thank you for allowing me to speak, instead of the perpetrators.

My testimony today is how the purification of thought has been accomplished by one company with a monopoly-like hold on the public commons in our internet era.

My name is **Jim Hoft** and I am the owner and editor of The Gateway Pundit (TGP) website based in St. Louis, Missouri.

I'm somewhat known in my business for my headlines. Here is the headline I bring to you: In the run-up to the 2016 election Americans got to choose what they read on Facebook. Today, Facebook chooses for them.

It is *your* constituents, left and right, rich and poor, who are impacted by this thought-filter imposed on what most believe is an unfiltered forum. It is they who are unknowingly cut off

from content they seek.

I grew up in Iowa, and I understand the pulse, the struggles, the hopes and dreams of Middle America. I came to find out Facebook doesn't like my type.

I launched Gateway Pundit in 2004 as a way to report on news that I didn't see the

MSM covering. At first, I had two or three daily readers, including my friend Chris and my twin brother, Joe. I was humbled and amazed to see our content grow in popularity over the years to nearly one million readers a

— 125 —

day thanks to promotions by Michelle Malkin, Glenn Reynolds, The Drudge Report and others. We provide news coverage and opinion that Americans could not find elsewhere.

There is no way to account for the demand for our content, on a shoestring budget we offered something the American people desired: **real news.** We were ranked by Harvard and Columbia Journalism Review as the 4th most influential conservative publisher in the 2016 election.[220]

Our readers: smart, patriotic, and diverse, have not given up on the promise of America. This is who I represent in speaking with you today.

2016 was a transformative election year.

This was the first election where Americans rejected, *en masse,* their legacy media options and turned to the freedom of choice and lack of filter on social media instead, through which they would share, comment on, and connect with content like mine.

We may not be invited to gala dinners and attend award shows, but our reporting is fulfilling a vital role of providing truthful content that is competition to the sanitized, on-message news of legacy media.

In fact, it was our readers who, on Election Day, were not surprised by the outcome.

The Gateway Pundit business cultivated its audience on Facebook, spending roughly $70,000 advertising on Facebook in 2015 resulting in 600,000 Facebook likes and supporters.

Over the past 19 months, Gateway Pundit saw a decline in our Facebook traffic from 24% of total website traffic in January 2017 to 2% of total website traffic in June 2018.

This is an 88% decrease in traffic from Facebook.

Recently we analyzed traffic numbers for some of the top conservative publishers in the U.S. **What we found was simply shocking.** Just as Gateway Pundit had been eliminated by Facebook from being seen by its

---

220 (Hoft J. , Harvard Study Identifies The Gateway Pundit As One of the Most Influential Conservative Media Outlets in 2016, 2017)

IN GOD WE TRUST

readers, **Facebook eliminated 93% of combined referral traffic to these websites from January 2017 to May 2018.**[221]

The site Western Journal and other conservative websites under their umbrella had more than *a billion* page views in 2016. Since then the organization lost 75% of its Facebook traffic. Likewise, Klicked Media, host of over 60 conservative websites, lost 400 million page views from Facebook in the last six months when compared to the prior year. **The total number of pageviews lost by just these two conservative online publishers is more than 1.5 billion pageviews from Facebook in one year.**[222]

After the 2016 election, Facebook began making algorithm changes to ensure conservative news was no longer an option for their users. Two studies released in March of 2018 confirm this. A study by The Outline Organization found conservative publishers were hit the hardest by recent Facebook algorithm changes -- and that The Gateway Pundit was hit the hardest.[223]

A Western Journal study in March revealed the same startling statistics. Further, this study found that liberal publishers actually saw a 2 percent increase in traffic.[224]

In fact, we found that every prominent conservative website from 2016 has either had their Facebook traffic diminished or entirely eliminated.[225]

If Facebook were seeking to hold a book burning, they wouldn't have been half as successful as they were in eliminating contrary points of view from being accessed by the American people.

In fact, book burning is benign when compared to what Facebook has silently done to restrict and eliminate diversity of thought; in book burnings, you can see the flames and watch the words disappear. In our case, we

---

221 (Hoft J. , SHOCK STUDY: Facebook Has Eliminated 93% of Traffic to Top Conservative Websites Since 2016 Election, 2018)

222 (Hoft J. , Top Conservative Publishers Speak Out: We Lost 1.5 Billion Facebook Pageviews Since 2016 Election, 2018)

223 (Martinaue, 2018)

224 (Hair, 2018)

225 (Hoft J. , Finally One Graphic Shows How Facebook Has Eliminated Conservative Content Since November 2016 Election (Click to Enlarge), 2018)

— 127 —

were silently and effectively "disappeared." Several top conservative sites have already closed their doors since 2017.

If our Fourth Estate is to remain an effective check as our Founders intended, we must ensure that the political purification of thoughts by one communication corporation, Facebook, is given ample competition. Today that competition is being eliminated. Tomorrow there will only be one sanctioned form of thought the American people will be allowed to hold.

This is not America.

BIBLIOGRAPHY

AP, R. a. (2016, November 2). *New York Times reports 95.7 percent fall in quarterly profit*. Retrieved from Dailymail.com: http://www.dailymail.co.uk/news/article-3897406/New-York-Times-reports-95-7-percent-fall-quarterly-profit.html?ito=email_share_article-top

Apelbaum, Y. (2020, February 7). *In God We Trust*. Retrieved from Apelbaum.word press.com: https://apelbaum.wordpress.com/2020/02/07/in-god-we-trust/

Apuzzo, M. S. (2015, July 24). *Inquiry Sought in Hillary Clinton's Use of Email*. Retrieved September 28, 2015, from NYTimes.com: http://www.nytimes.com/2015/07/24/us/politics/inquiry-is-sought-in-hillary-clinton-email-account.html

Archer, C. C. (2012, November 28). *Cox and Archer: Why $16 Trillion Only Hints at the True U.S. Debt*. Retrieved October 19, 2014, from Onlinewsj. com: http://online.wsj.com/news/articles/SB10001424127887323353204578127374039087636?mg=reno64-wsj&url=http%3A%2F%2Fonline.wsj.com%2Farticle%2FSB10001424127887323353204578127374039087636.html

Bank, W. (2019, December 5). *China GDP*. Retrieved from TradingEconomics.com: https://tradingeconomics.com/china/gdp

Bank, W. (2019, December 5). *US GDP*. Retrieved from TradingEconomics.com: https://tradingeconomics.com/united-states/gdp

Bedard, P. (2014, October 6). *Gallup: Voter opposition to Obama at 16-year high, worse than Bush, Clinton*. Retrieved January 3, 2015, from Washington Examiner.com: http://www.washingtonexaminer.com/gallup-voter-opposition-to-obama-at-16-year-high-worse-than-bush-clinton/article/2554404#!

Bedard, P. (2016, June 17). *A first: More workers at online sites than newspapers.* Retrieved June 18, 2016, from WashingtonExaminer.com: http://www.washing tonexaminer.com/a-first-more-workers-at-online-sites-than-newspapers/ article/2594197

Blog-Global-Research, W. (2014, April 26). *Confirmed: U.S. Armed Al Qaeda to Topple Libya's Gaddaffi.* Retrieved December 30, 2014, from GlobalResearch.ca: http://www.globalresearch.ca/confirmed-u-s-armed-al-qaeda-to-topple-libyas-gaddaffi/5379301

Bloomberg. (2018, September 3). *There's Not-So-Good News Buried in China Developers' Fabulous Earnings.* Retrieved from Bloomberg.com: https:// www.bloomberg.com/news/articles/2018-09-02/not-so-good-news-buried-in-china-developers-fabulous-earnings

Board, N. E. (2015, August 16). *HIllary Clinton's 5 email lies.* Retrieved September 28, 2015, from NYPost: http://nypost.com/2015/08/16/ hillary-clintons-5-e-mail-lies/

Bruce, T. (2015, February 5). *FCC, FEC look to ruin the Internet.* Retrieved February 21, 2015, from WashingtonTimes.com: http://www.washington-times.com/news/2015/feb/16/tammy-bruce-fcc-fec-look-ruin-internet/

Bruggeman, J. H. (2018, June 8). *'Oconus lures': Evolution of a conspiracy theory, from Reddit to the White House.* Retrieved from ABCNews.go.com: https://abcnews.go.com/Politics/oconus-lures-evolution-conspiracy-theory-reddit-white-house/story?id=55730297

Byers, D. (2015, February 13). *Brian Williams' alleged lies: A list.* Retrieved February 20, 2015, from Politico.com: http://www.politico.com/blogs/ media/2015/02/brian-williams-alleged-lies-a-list-202585.html

Caplan, J. (2017, November 4). *MATT DRUDGE TWEETS: Donna Brazile 'Haunted' By Seth Rich Murder — Feared Snipers Would Kill Her Next.* Retrieved from TheGatewayPundit.com: https://www.thegatewaypundit.com/2017/11/matt-drudge-tweets-donna-brazile-haunted-seth-rich-murder-feared-snipers-kill-next/

Caralle, K. (2019, November 18). *Jerome Powell forced to issue statement saying the Fed will make its decisions solely based on 'non-political' analysis after being summoned to the White House by Trump.* Retrieved from Dailymail.com: https://www.dailymail.co.uk/news/article-7698637/Fed-chief-reasserts-independence-talks-Trump.html

Carlson, J. (2018, May 21). *John Carlin – The Former NSD Head Who Enabled the FBI's Carter Page FISA Warrant.* Retrieved from TheMarketsWork.com: https://themarketswork.com/2018/05/21/john-carlin-the-former-nsd-head-who-enabled-the-fbis-carter-page-fisa-warrant/

Carroll, C. (2014, August 26). *If Obama's Bombing of Libya Was Legal, His Bombing of Syria Would Be Too.* Retrieved December 30, 2014, from Townhall.com: http://townhall.com/tipsheet/conncarroll/2014/08/26/when-does-obamas-n1883363

Cassidy, M. (2016, December 15). *Arpaio: Probe proves Obama birth certificate is 'fake'.* Retrieved from AZCentral.com: https://www.azcentral.com/story/news/local/phoenix/2016/12/15/sheriff-joe-arpaio-5-year-investigation-proves-obama-birth-certificate-fake/95444730/

Cassidy, M. (2017, July 31). *Arpaio found guilty of criminal contempt.* Retrieved from AZCentral.com: https://www.azcentral.com/story/news/local/phoenix/2017/07/31/maricopa-county-sheriff-joe-arpaio-found-guilty-criminal-contempt-court/486278001/

Chantrill, C. (2014, October 19). *Government Spending in United States.* Retrieved October 19, 2014, from USgovernmentspending.com: http://www.usgovernmentspending.com/

Cooke, J. L. (2016, November 15). *Google, Facebook move to restrict ads on fake news sites.* Retrieved from Reuters.com: http://www.reuters.com/article/us-alphabet-advertising-idUSKBN1392MM

Coulter, A. (2003). *Slander.* New York City: Three Rivers Press.

Creitz, C. (2019, Septermber 8). *Dr. Robert Epstein: Study claims Google reflected 'very dramatic bias' in 2016 election search results.* Retrieved from FOXNews.com: https://www.foxnews.com/media/google-bias-search-results-trump-clinton-epstein-levin

DailySource.org. (2014, November 29). *Current Problems in the Media.* Retrieved December 14, 2014, from DailySource.org: http://www.dailysource.org/about/problems#.VIwoW5bXfCQ

Dang, S. (2019, June 5). *Google, Facebook have tight grip on growing U.S. online ad market: report.* Retrieved from Reuters.com: https://www.reuters.com/article/us-alphabet-facebook-advertising/google-facebook-have-tight-grip-on-growing-u-s-online-ad-market-report-idUSKCN1T61IV

Davis, S. (2015, April 29). *Is The Clinton Foundation Just An International Money Laundering Scheme?* Retrieved October 4, 2015, from TheFederalist.com: http://thefederalist.com/2015/04/29/is-the-clinton-foundation-just-an-international-money-laundering-scheme/

Dodge, B. (2019, December 20). *Americans' Positive Views on the Economy Could Earn Trump a Boost in 2020, New Poll Suggests.* Retrieved from Newsweek.com: https://www.newsweek.com/best-economy-scores-since-2001-could-earn-trump-boost-2020-new-poll-cnn-1478567

IN GOD WE TRUST

Dumpala, P. (2009, July 4). *The Year The Newspaper Died.* Retrieved December 22, 2014, from BusinessInsider.com: http://www.businessinsider.com/the-death-of-the-american-newspaper-2009-7?op=1

Dunleavy, J. (2019, September 25). *READ: White House transcript of Trump call with Ukrainian president.* Retrieved from WashingtonExaminer.com: https://www.washingtonexaminer.com/news/read-white-house-transcript-of-trumps-call-with-ukraines-president

Durden, T. (2015, January 1). *For CNBC, 2014 Was The Worst. Year. Ever.* Retrieved January 3, 2015, from Zerohedge.com: http://www.zerohedge.com/news/2015-01-01/cnbc-2014-was-worst-year-ever

Emanuel, M. (2014, August 29). *Census figures show more than one-third of Americans receiving welfare benefits.* Retrieved October 21, 2014, from Foxnews.com: http://www.foxnews.com/politics/2014/08/29/census-figures-show-more-than-one-third-americans-receiving-welfare-benefits/

Evens-Pritchard, A. (2015, January 20). *Central bank prophet fears QE warfare pushing world financial system out of control.* Retrieved January 26, 2015, from Telegraph.co.uk: http://www.telegraph.co.uk/finance/economics/11358316/Central-bank-prophet-fears-QE-warfare-pushing-world-financial-system-out-of-control.html

Fakkert, J. (2018, March 15). *Unlawful FISA Spying Widespread Under Obama Administration.* Retrieved from EpochTimes.com: https://www.theepochtimes.com/fisa-abuse-widespread-under-obama-administration-2_2465325.html

Fazzini, K. (2019, April 18). *Mueller report details how Russians reached millions of US Facebook and Twitter users and brought them out to real-life rallies.* Retrieved from CNBC.com: https://www.cnbc.com/2019/04/18/mueller-report-details-social-media-organizing-that-reached-americans.html

Flynn, M. (2014, October 12). *US Slips to 12th in Economic Freedom*. Retrieved October 18, 2014, from Breitbart.com: http://www.breitbart.com/Big-Government/2014/10/10/US-Slips-to-12th-in-Economic-Freedom

FNA. (2014, December 14). *Bill Ayers: The United States Is the Foremost Threat to World Peace Today*. Retrieved December 20, 2014, from Farsnews.com: http://english.farsnews.com/newstext.aspx?nn=13930915000040

Foundation, T. C. (n.d.). *About*. Retrieved September 28, 2015, from The ClintonFoundation: https://www.clintonfoundation.org/about

Foxnews.com. (2014, December 6). *China surpasses U.S. to become largest world economy*. Retrieved December 7, 2014, from Foxnews.com: http://www.foxnews.com/world/2014/12/06/china-surpasses-us-to-become-largest-world-economy/

Fund, J. (2014, December 22). *Obama Support among Military Plummets to 15 Percent*. Retrieved January 25, 2015, from NatiionalReview.com: http://www.nationalreview.com/corner/395212/obama-support-among-military-plummets-15-percent-john-fund

Garrow, D. (2003, March 27). *The Tragedy of William O. Douglas*. Retrieved August 1, 2015, from thenation.com: http://www.thenation.com/article/tragedy-william-o-douglas/

Gillespie, P. (2014, October 16). *Over 48 million Americans live in poverty*. Retrieved October 26, 2014, from Money.CNN.com: http://money.cnn.com/2014/10/16/news/economy/48-million-americans-poverty-census-bureau/

Grassley, C. (2018, February 12). *Grassley, Graham Uncover 'Unusual Email' Sent by Susan Rice to Herself on President Trump's Inauguration Day*. Retrieved from Grassley.

Senate.gov: https://www.grassley.senate.gov/news/news-releases/grassley-graham-uncover-unusual-email-sent-susan-rice-herself-president-trump-s

Griffing, J. (2009, September 1). *The Prince of Lies*. Retrieved December 20, 2014, from AmericanThinker.com: http://www.americanthinker.com/articles/2009/09/the_prince_of_lies.html

Grusky, D. B. (2014). *State of the Union: The Stanford Center of Poverty and Inequality: The Poverty and Inequality Report - 2014*. Retrieved October 26, 2014, from Web.Stanford.edu: http://web.stanford.edu/group/scspi/sotu/SOTU_2014_CPI.pdf

Hair, G. U. (2018, March 13). *Confirmed: Facebook's Recent Algorithm Change Is Crushing Conservative Sites, Boosting Liberals*. Retrieved from WesternJournal.com: https://www.westernjournal.com/confirmed-facebooks-recent-algorithm-change-is-crushing-conservative-voices-boosting-liberals/

Hanson, V. D. (2019, December 20). *Victor Davis Hanson: Former intelligence chiefs fit perfectly into media advocacy culture*. Retrieved from FOXNews.com: https://www.foxnews.com/opinion/victor-davis-hanson-former-intelligence-chiefs-fit-perfectly-into-media-advocacy-culture

Harress, C. (2013, December 2). *Who Is The Longest-Serving Federal Reserve Chairman In History?* Retrieved February 10, 2015, from IBTimes.com: http://www.ibtimes.com/who-longest-serving-federal-reserve-chairman-history-1491906

Hemingway, M. (2019, December 10). *IG Report Confirms Schiff FISA Memo Media Praised Was Riddled With Lies*. Retrieved from TheFederalist.com: https://thefederalist.com/2019/12/10/ig-report-confirms-schiff-fisa-memo-media-praised-was-riddled-with-lies/

Henley, W. (2012, November 28). *The Loss of the Fourth Estate and the Threat to American Liberty.* Retrieved November 29, 2014, from Christianpost.com: http://www.christianpost.com/news/the-loss-of-the-fourth-estate-and-the-threat-to-american-liberty-85644/

Herridge, J. B. (2015, March 6). *Clinton's personal email use – despite clear rules – raises double-standard questions.* Retrieved October 4, 2015, from Foxnews.com: http://www.foxnews.com/politics/2015/03/06/clintons-personal-email-use-despite-clear-rules-raises-double-standard/#.VPszeuW78Xg. mailto

Hoft, J. (2016, November 4). *Election Prediction 2016: Current Trend Lines Show Trump Will Win in Landslide.* Retrieved from TheGatewayPundit.com: https://www.thegatewaypundit.com/2016/11/2016-election-tgp-prediction-trump-wins-by-landslide/

Hoft, J. (2017, September 10). *Harvard Study Identifies The Gateway Pundit As One of the Most Influential Conservative Media Outlets in 2016.* Retrieved from TheGatewayPundit.com: https://www.thegatewaypundit.com/2017/09/another-election-analysis-identifies-the-gateway-pundit-as-the-4th-most-influential-right-leaning-media-outlet-during-2016-election/

Hoft, J. (2018, June 4). *Breaking: Senate Releases Unredacted Strzok-Page Texts Showing FBI Initiated MULTIPLE SPIES in Trump Campaign in December 2015.* Retrieved from TheGatewayPundit.com: https://www.thegatewaypundit.com/2018/06/breaking-senate-releases-unredacted-strzok-page-texts-showing-fbi-initiated-multiple-spies-in-trump-campaign-in-december-2015/

Hoft, J. (2018, September 4). *Finally One Graphic Shows How Facebook Has Eliminated Conservative Content Since November 2016 Election (Click to Enlarge).* Retrieved from TheGatewayPundit.com: https://www.thegatewaypundit.

IN GOD WE TRUST

com/2018/09/finally-one-graphic-shows-how-facebook-has-eliminated-conservative-content-since-the-election-of-donald-trump/

Hoft, J. (2018, October 15). *Joe Hoft and John Schlafly Discuss The Top 10 Reasons the Mueller Investigation Is Unconstitutional (Video).* Retrieved from TheGatewayPundit.com: https://www.thegatewaypundit.com/2018/10/joe-hoft-and-john-schlafly-discuss-the-top-10-reasons-the-mueller-investigation-is-unconstitutional-video/

Hoft, J. (2018, August 31). *NEVER FORGET: Dirty Cop Mueller Gave Tony Podesta Immunity to Testify Against Manafort After Committing Same Exact Crime.* Retrieved from TheGatewayPundit.com: https://www.thegatewaypundit.com/2018/08/never-forget-dirty-cop-mueller-gave-tony-podesta-immunity-to-testify-against-manafort-after-committing-same-exact-crime/

Hoft, J. (2018, July 17). *SHOCK STUDY: Facebook Has Eliminated 93% of Traffic to Top Conservative Websites Since 2016 Election.* Retrieved from TheGatewayPundit.com: https://www.thegatewaypundit.com/2018/07/shock-study-facebook-has-eliminated-93-of-traffic-to-top-conservative-websites-since-2016-election/

Hoft, J. (2018, August 30). *Top Conservative Publishers Speak Out: We Lost 1.5 Billion Facebook Pageviews Since 2016 Election.* Retrieved from TheGatewayPundit.com: https://www.thegatewaypundit.com/2018/08/top-conservative-publishers-speak-out-we-lost-1-5-billion-facebook-pageviews-since-2016-election/

Hoft, J. (2019, March 22). *After 675 Days of Witch Hunt: More Than 80% of Mueller Indictments Were of Russian Actors Who Will Never See US Courtroom.* Retrieved from TheGatewayPundit.com: https://www.thegatewaypundit.com/2019/03/after-675-days-of-witch-hunt-more-than-80-of-mueller-junk-indictments-were-of-russian-actors-who-will-never-see-us-courtroom/

Hoft, J. (2019, March 1). *At Least FIVE TIMES Dirty Cop Mueller and Andrew Weissmann Created Crimes that Resulted in Indictments of Thousands of Innocent Individuals and Companies*. Retrieved from TheGatewayPundit.com: https://www.thegatewaypundit.com/2019/03/at-least-five-times-dirty-cop-mueller-and-andrew-weissmann-created-crimes-that-resulted-in-indictments-of-thousands-of-innocent-individuals-and-companies/

Hoft, J. (2019, April 29). *COMPLETE BS: Jared Kushner Explains How Mueller's Junk Report of Russian Facebook Influence Was Deep State Garbage*. Retrieved from TheGatewayPundit.com: https://www.thegatewaypundit.com/2019/04/complete-bs-jared-kushner-explains-how-muellers-junk-report-of-russian-facebook-influence-was-deep-state-garbage/

Hoft, J. (2019, June 4). *Esteemed NSA Whistleblower Bill Binney Says He Has Evidence DNC was NOT Hacked – "The Mueller Report and the Rosenstein Indictment Is All Based on Lies!"*. Retrieved from TheGatewayPundit.com: https://www.thegatewaypundit.com/2019/06/esteemed-nsa-whistleblower-bill-binney-says-he-has-evidence-dnc-was-not-hacked-the-mueller-report-and-the-rosenstein-indictment-is-all-based-on-lies/

Hoft, J. (2019, December 2). *Four Were Hanged In 1865 Democrat Coup Involving Lincoln's Assassination – None from 2016 Democrat Coup to Take Out Trump*. Retrieved from TheGatewayPundit.com: https://www.thegatewaypundit.com/2019/12/four-were-hung-in-1865-democrat-coup-involving-lincolns-assassination-none-from-2016-democrat-coup-to-take-out-trump/

Hoft, J. (2019, June 26). *MAJOR FIND: More Ammunition for Roger Stone: The Only Firm to Review DNC Server, Crowdstrike, is Connected to James Clapper, The Atlantic Council and More Shoddy IT Investigative Work*. Retrieved from TheGatewayPundit.com: https://www.thegatewaypundit.com/2019/06/major-find-more-ammunition-for-roger-stone-the-only-firm-to-review-dnc-server-crowdstrike-is-connected-to-james-clapper-the-atlantic-council-and-more-shoddy-it-investigative-work/

Hoft, J. (2019, September 12). *MUST READ... Evidence Suggests Deep State Asset Joseph Mifsud Was One of the Spies (Oconus Lores) Referred to in Strzok-Page Texts from December 2015.* Retrieved from TheGatewayPundit.com: https://www.thegatewaypundit.com/wp-admin/post.php?post=457968&action=edit

Hoft, J. (2019, August 24). *MUST READ... TRUMP IS RIGHT! China Is In Terrible Economic Condition; Cannot Afford to Lose the US Market.* Retrieved from TheGatewayPundit.com: https://www.thegatewaypundit.com/2019/08/must-read-trump-is-right-china-is-in-terrible-economic-condition-cannot-afford-to-lose-the-us-market/

Hoft, J. (2019, February 25). *New Documentary of Robert Mueller Starring Attorney Robert Barnes Shows "He's No Patriot!".* Retrieved from TheGatewayPundit.com: https://www.thegatewaypundit.com/2019/02/documentary-of-robert-mueller-shows-hes-no-patriot/

Hoft, J. (2019, March 8). *THE LIST: More than 100 Times the FBI, DOJ and/or Mueller Gang "Deviated from Standard Practice" or Committed Crimes in Effort to Exonerate Hillary and Indict Trump.* Retrieved from TheGatewayPundit.com: https://www.thegatewaypundit.com/2019/03/the-list-more-than-100-times-the-fbi-doj-and-or-mueller-gang-deviated-from-standard-practice-or-committed-crimes-in-effort-to-exonerate-hilary-and-indict-trump/

Hoft, J. (2019, 11 27). *Want Evidence the Fed Stalled the Trump Rally? 11 of Past 19 Days Since the Fed Lowered the Fed Funds Rate the DOW Hit All-Time Highs.* Retrieved from TheGatewayPundit.com: https://www.thegatewaypundit.com/2019/11/want-evidence-the-fed-stalled-the-trump-rally-11-of-past-19-days-since-the-fed-lowered-the-fed-funds-rate-the-dow-hit-all-time-highs/

Hoft, J. (2019, October 19). *Winning, Winning, Winning! President Trump Decreases Debt to GDP Ratio Indicating Economy Growing Faster than US Debt!* Retrieved from TheGatewayPundit.com: https://www.thegatewaypundit.

com/2019/10/winning-winning-winning-president-trump-decreases-debt-to-gdp-ratio-indicating-economy-growing-faster-than-us-debt/

Hoft, J. (2020, January 30). *BREAKING EXCLUSIVE: FBI Covered Up Strzok and Page Emails Regarding Seth Rich — Now the FBI Is Doubling Down In their Cover-Up.* Retrieved from TheGatewayPundit.com: https://www.thegatewaypundit.com/2020/01/breaking-exclusive-fbi-covered-up-strzok-and-page-emails-regarding-seth-rich-now-the-fbi-is-doubling-down-in-their-cover-up/

House.gov. (n.d.). *Record Holders.* Retrieved August 1, 2015, from House.gov: http://history.house.gov/Institution/Firsts-Milestones/Record-Holders/

HRW. (2012). *World Report 2012: China.* Retrieved October 16, 2014, from Hrw. org: http://www.hrw.org/world-report-2012/world-report-2012-china

Jacobson, L. (2017, February 17). *Did Donald Trump inherit 'a mess' from Barack Obama?* Retrieved from Politifact.com: https://www.politifact.com/truth-o-meter/article/2017/feb/17/did-donald-trump-inherit-mess/

James Gwartney, R. L. (2019, September 12). *Economic Freedom of the World 2019 Annual Report.* Retrieved from Fraserinstitute.org: https://www.fraserinstitute.org/sites/default/files/economic-freedom-of-the-world-2019-execsum.pdf

Johnson, J. T. (2017, May 17). *Former FBI Director Mueller Appointed As Special Counsel To Oversee Russia Probe.* Retrieved from NPR.org: https://www.npr.org/2017/05/17/528846598/former-fbi-director-mueller-appointed-special-counsel-to-oversee-russia-probe

Justice, O. o. (2019, December 9). *Review of Four FISA Applications and Other Aspects of the FBI's Crossfire Hurricane Investigation.* Retrieved from Justice.gov: https://www.justice.gov/storage/120919-examination.pdf

Krugman, P. (2016, November 9). *The Economic Fallout.* Retrieved from NewYorkTimes.com: https://www.nytimes.com/interactive/projects/cp/opinion/election-night-2016/paul-krugman-the-economic-fallout

Laila, C. (2019, June 14). *FIGURES. FBI/DOJ Never Obtained the Unredacted CrowdStrike Reports on 'Russian Hack' of DNC Servers.* Retrieved from TheGatewayPundit.com: https://www.thegatewaypundit.com/2019/06/figures-fbi-doj-never-obtained-the-unredacted-crowdstrike-reports-on-russian-hack-of-dnc-server/

Lalia, C. (2017, May 16). *FLASHBACK=>John Podesta: 'I'm Definitely For Making an Example of a Suspected Leaker'.* Retrieved from The GatewayPundit.com: https://www.thegatewaypundit.com/2017/05/flashbackjohn-podesta-im-definitely-making-example-suspected-leaker/

Levin, M. (2013). *Liberty Amendments.* New York: Threshold Editiions.

Lines, T. F. (2020, January 22). *CrowdStrike's work with the Democratic National Committee: Setting the record straight.* Retrieved from Crowdstrike.com: https://www.crowdstrike.com/blog/bears-midst-intrusion-democratic-national-committee/

Mardell, M. (2015, February 9). *BBC Radio 4: World at One: Alan Greenspan: "I'm afraid (the US is) going to run into some form of political crisis".* Retrieved February 10, 2015, from BBC.co.uk: http://www.bbc.co.uk/programmes/p02jmyh5

Martens, P. M. (2015, February 5). *Gallup CEC Fears He Might "Suddenly Disappear" for Questioning US Jobs Data.* Retrieved February 20, 2015, from WallStreetParade.com: http://wallstreetonparade.com/2015/02/gallup-ceo-fears-he-might-suddenly-disappear-for-questioning-u-s-jobs-data/

Martin, W. (2018, October 17). *China's Hidden $6 Trillion Debt Pile Is an Iceberg Posing a Titanic Risk.* Retrieved from Businessinsider.com: https://www.

businessinsider.com/china-debt-crisis-6-trillion-off-balance-sheet-debt-poses-titanic-risk-2018-10

Martinaue, P. (2018, March 5). *Conservative Publishers Hit Hardest by Facebook News Feed Change*. Retrieved from TheOutline.com: https://theoutline.com/post/3599/conservative-publishers-hit-hardest-by-facebook-news-feed-change

Mayer, J. (2011, May 23). *The Secret Sharer*. Retrieved from NewYorker.com: https://www.newyorker.com/magazine/2011/05/23/the-secret-sharer

McGlothlin, J. (2014, September 19). *Gallup Poll: Trust In Media At All Time Low*. Retrieved December 17, 2014, from Westernjournalism.com: http://www.westernjournalism.com/gallup-poll-trust-media-time-low/#eHFsH1WStx6USfOO.03

Mendolera, K. (2012, January 12). *152 newspapers shut down in 2011*. Retrieved December 22, 2014, from PRDaily.com: http://www.prdaily.com/Main/Articles/152_newspapers_shut_down_in_2011_10536.aspx

Meyer, A. (2014, December 5). *Labor Force Participation Remains at 36-Year Low*. Retrieved December 7, 2014, from CNSNews.com: http://www.cnsnews.com/news/article/ali-meyer/labor-force-participation-remains-36-year-low-0

Mills, D. (2017, June 8). *Full Transcript and Video: James Comey's Testimony on Capitol Hill*. Retrieved from NYTimes.com: https://www.nytimes.com/2017/06/08/us/politics/senate-hearing-transcript.html

Moore, J. (2015, January 4). *Second Release GOP Results 1-4-15*. Retrieved January 18, 2015, from Scribd.com: http://www.scribd.com/doc/251627101/Second-release-gop-Results-1-4-15

IN GOD WE TRUST

Newman, A. (2014, May 5). *Poll: Most Americans View Feds as Threat to Liberty - See more at: http://truthviamedia.net/news-of-amerika/poll-most-americans-view-feds-as-threat-to-liberty/#sthash.wbH70zwD.dpuf.* Retrieved January 25, 2015, from TruthviaMedia.com: http://truthviamedia.net/news-of-amerika/poll-most-americans-view-feds-as-threat-to-liberty/

Nolte, J. (2013, September 7). *CNN, CBS News, ABC News Honchos Have Obama Administration Family Ties.* Retrieved October 25, 2015, from Breitbart.com: http://www.breitbart.com/big-journalism/2013/09/07/mainstream-media-honchos-related-towhite-house-officials/

Nolte, J. (2014, September 30). *Fox News Slaughters CNN, MSNBC; Hits Historic Ratings Milestone.* Retrieved January 3, 2015, from Breitbart.com: http://www.breitbart.com/big-journalism/2014/09/30/fox-slaughters-msnbc-cnn-ratings-milestone/

Noyes, R. (2014, September 8). *MRC Study: TV Buries the Bad News on Obama's Collapsing Polls.* Retrieved November 30, 2014, from Newsbusters.org: http://newsbusters.org/blogs/rich-noyes/2014/09/08/mrc-study-tv-buries-bad-news-obamas-collapsing-polls

Noyes, R. (2017, December 12). *Even As Media Whine About Trump, Their Hostile Coverage Shows No Let Up.* Retrieved from Newsbusters.com: https://www.newsbusters.org/blogs/nb/rich-noyes/2017/12/12/even-media-whine-about-trump-their-hostile-coverage-shows-no-let

O'Brien, C. (2014, December 29). *Hm: Only Three Democrats Make GQ's 'Craziest Politicians' List.* Retrieved December 30, 2014, from Townhall.com: http://townhall.com/tipsheet/cortneyobrien/2014/12/29/only-3-democrats-make-gqs-craziest-politicians-list-n1936557#!

Pergram, C. (2014, February 24). *Democratic Rep. Dingell, longest-serving congressman, to retire.* Retrieved August 1, 2015, from FOXNews.com:

http://www.foxnews.com/politics/2014/02/24/democratic-rep-dingell-longest-serving-congressman-to-retire/

Perlez, P. M. (2014, December 1). *Gregorious and Direct: China's Web Doorkeeper*. Retrieved December 8, 2014, from NYTimes.com: http://www.nytimes.com/2014/12/02/world/asia/gregarious-and-direct-chinas-web-door keeper.html?_r=1

Podhoretz, J. (2016, May 5). *White House Admits It Played Us for Fools to Sell Iran Deal*. Retrieved May 7, 2016, from NYPost.com: http://nypost.com/2016/05/05/playing-the-press-and-the-public-for-chumps-to-sell-the-iran-deal/

Powe, A. (2018, June 14). *Attorney Warns: Aaron Rich Refuses to Authorize Wikileaks To Reveal Info on Seth Rich*. Retrieved from TheGatewayPundit.com: https://www.thegatewaypundit.com/2018/06/attorney-warns-rich-fam-ily-obama-admin-lawyers-desperately-obstructing-wikileaks-from-reveal-ing-truth-about-hacked-dnc-server/

Reynolds, G. (2016, May 22). *Glenn Reynolds: When leaders cheat, followers ... follow*. Retrieved May 29, 2016, from USAToday.com: http://www.usatoday.com/story/opinion/2016/05/22/government-corruption-law-abiding-society-trust-irs-hillary-clinton-column/84744432/

RFE/RL. (n.d.). *Then And Now: Free Media In Unfree Societies*. Retrieved October 4, 2014, from Radio Free Europe; Radio Liberty: http://www.rferl.org/info/history/133.html

Rhodan, M. (2016, July 5). *Read FBI Director James Comey's Speech on the Hillary Clinton Email Probe*. Retrieved from Time.com: https://time.com/4393372/james-comey-fbi-hillary-clinton-email-speech-transcript/

Rich, H. (2011, April 15). *Rasmussenreports.com*. Retrieved October 12, 2014, from New Media Catches Obama Bribing the Fourth Estate:

IN GOD WE TRUST

http://www.rasmussenreports.com/public_content/political_com
mentary/commentary_by_howard_rich/new_media_catches_obama_
bribing_the_fourth_estate

Rid, T. (2016, July 25). *All Signs Point to Russia Being Behind the DNC Hack*.
Retrieved from Vice.com: https://www.vice.com/en_us/article/4xa5g9/
all-signs-point-to-russia-being-behind-the-dnc-hack

Riggs, M. (2010, June 28). *Sen. Robert Byrd not only was a KKK member but led his
local Klan chapter*. Retrieved August 1, 2015, from Dailycaller.com: http://
dailycaller.com/2010/06/28/sen-robert-byrd-not-only-was-a-kkk-mem-
ber-but-led-his-local-klan-chapter/

Riley, N. S. (2014, November 29). *CNN is Lying when They say Ferguson
Protests were 'Peaceful'*. Retrieved December 9, 2014, from NYPost.com:
http://nypost.com/2014/11/29/why-cnn-wants-you-to-believe-the-
ferguson-protests-were-peaceful/

Rodriguez, K. (2019, September 8). *6.2 Million Individuals Off Food Stamps
Under Trump*. Retrieved from Breitbart.com: https://www.breitbart.com/
economy/2019/09/08/6-2-million-individuals-off-food-stamps-under-
trump/

Rose, N. (2014, August 29). *OUTRAGEOUS: New Report Reveals Obama And
Holder Are Abusing Power To Fund Radical Liberal Groups*. Retrieved December
24, 2014, from WesternJournalism.com: http://www.westernjournalism.
com/outrage-obama-holder-running-a-big-money-laundering-racket-to-
fund-radical-left/#oEMiYUiewxlz5B28.97

Rosenberg, A. (2015, January 29). *Reagan's OMB head: Wealth inequality is a
problem*. Retrieved January 30, 2015, from CNBC.com: http://www.cnbc.
com/id/102381666

— 145 —

Saad, L. (2015, January 2). *Cluster of Concerns Vie for Top U.S. Problem in 2014.* Retrieved January 18, 2015, from Gallup.com: http://www.gallup.com/poll/180398/cluster-concerns-vie-top-problem-2014.aspx

Schwartz, N. D. (2014, December 5). *Big Job Gains and Raising Pay in Labor Data.* Retrieved December 7, 2014, from NYTimes.com: http://www.nytimes.com/2014/12/06/business/economy/november-jobs-unemployment-figures.html?_r=0

Schweizer, P. (2013). *Extortion - How Politicians Extract your Money, Buy Votes, and Line Their Own Pockets.* Boston: Houghton Mifflin Harcourt.

Senate.gov. (2015, May 13). *Longest Serving.* Retrieved August 1, 2015, from Senate.gov: http://www.senate.gov/senators/Biographical/longest_serving.htm

Sessions, D. (2011, March 24). *Did Obama Write His Own Memoirs?* Retrieved December 20, 2014, from TheDailyBeast.com: http://www.thedailybeast.com/articles/2011/03/24/jack-cashills-deconstructing-obama-argues-bill-ayers-wrote-obamas-memoirs.html#

Shapiro, B. (2014, August 27). *Dozens of Businesses Move HQs Outside America Under Obama.* Retrieved October 26, 2014, from Breitbart.com: http://www.breitbart.com/Big-Government/2014/08/27/businesses-move-inversion

Shaw, J. (2015, September 27). *Video: Hillary's flailing attempt to explain the email scandal to Chuck Todd.* Retrieved September 27, 2015, from Hotair.com: http://hotair.com/archives/2015/09/27/video-hillarys-flailing-attempt-to-explain-the-email-scandal-to-chuck-todd/

Silva, C. D. (2019, September 26). *Adam Schiff Faces Backlash For Parodying Donald Trump's Ukraine Call During Congressional Hearing: 'What A Hack'.* Retrieved from Newsweek.com: https://www.newsweek.com/adam-schiff-parody-

IN GOD WE TRUST

donald-trump-congressional-hearing-whistleblower-complaint-ukraine-call-1461579

Smith, K. (2014, October 25). *Ex CBS Reporter's Book Reveals How Liberal Media Protects Obama.* Retrieved October 25, 2015, from NYPost.com: http://nypost.com/2014/10/25/former-cbs-reporter-explains-how-the-liberal-media-protects-obama/

Statistics, B. o. (2019, December 7). *Databases, Tables & Calculators by Subject.* Retrieved from BLS.gov: https://data.bls.gov/timeseries/CES0000000001?output_view=net_1mth

Sundance. (2019, July 15). *Lawsuit Claims Julian Assange Confirmed DNC Emails Received From Seth Rich—Not a Russian Hack....* Retrieved from The Conservative Treehouse. com: https://theconservativetreehouse.com/2019/07/15/lawsuit-claims-julian-assange-confirmed-dnc-emails-received-from-seth-rich-not-a-russian-hack/

Supremecourt.gov. (2010, August). *Faq_Justices.* Retrieved August 1, 2015, from Supremecourt.gov: http://www.supremecourt.gov/faq_justices.aspx

System, B. o. (2020, January 12). *Federal Reserve History.* Retrieved from FederalReserve.gov: https://www.federalreserve.gov/aboutthefed/centennial/about.htm

System, T. B. (2020, January 11). *The Board of Governors of the Federal Reserve System.* Retrieved from FederalReserve.gov: https://www.federalreserve.gov/monetarypolicy/openmarket.htm

Thee-Brenan, A. R. (2014, December 11). *Many Feel the American Dream Is Out of Reach, Poll Shows.* Retrieved December 11, 2014, from NYTimes.com: http://dealbook.nytimes.com/2014/12/10/many-feel-the-american-dream-is-out-of-reach-poll-shows/?_r=0

Time.com. (n.d.). *Complete List: Conspiracy Theories*. Retrieved December 14, 2014, from Time.com: http://content.time.com/time/specials/packages/completelist/0,29569,1860871,00.html

Trump, D. J. (2018, June 6). *@realdonaldtrump*. Retrieved from Twitter.com: https://twitter.com/realDonaldTrump/status/1004160401658073090?ref_src=twsrc%5Etfw%7Ctwcamp%5Etweetembed%7Ctwterm%5E1004160401658073090&ref_url=https%3A%2F%2Fwww.thegateway-pundit.com%2Fwp-admin%2Fpost.php%3Fpost%3D457968%26action%3Dedit

Trump, D. J. (2019, December 22). *@realdonaldtrump*. Retrieved from Twitter.com: https://twitter.com/realDonaldTrump/status/1208873492025925632

Trump, D. J. (2019, August 23). *@realdonaldtrump*. Retrieved from Twitter.com: https://twitter.com/realDonaldTrump/status/1164914610836783104

Trump, D. J. (2019, November 18). *@realdonaldtrump*. Retrieved from Twitter.com: https://twitter.com/realDonaldTrump/status/1196458467982270464

Trump, D. J. (2019, November 18). *@realdonaldtrump*. Retrieved from Twitter.com: https://twitter.com/realDonaldTrump/status/1196632739266596865

Unruh, B. (2016, October 1). *Obama-appointed judge lets Internet giveaway proceed*. Retrieved from WND.com: http://www.wnd.com/2016/09/obama-appointed-judge-lets-internet-giveaway-proceed/

Weaver, L. W. (2014). *Indiana.edu*. Retrieved October 16, 2014, from The American Journalist in the Digital Age: Key Findings: http://news.indiana.edu/releases/iu/2014/05/2013-american-journalist-key-findings.pdf

IN GOD WE TRUST

Welsh, M. (2015, April 15). *Tax Calculator: The federal debt*. Retrieved October 24, 2015, from FoxNews.com: http://www.foxnews.com/politics/2015/04/15/tax-calculator-federal-debt/#.VS5_J-hMOeE.mailto

Wheeler, B. (2013, October 23). *Are conspiracy theories destroying democracy?* Retrieved December 14, 2014, from BBC.com: http://www.bbc.com/news/uk-politics-24650841

Williamson, K. D. (2014, December 23). *The IRS: Just One of Dozens of Uncooperative Agencies*. Retrieved December 30, 2014, from NationalReview.com: http://www.nationalreview.com/article/395337/irs-just-one-dozens-uncooperative-agencies-kevin-d-williamson/page/0/1

Wolff, J. (2017, May 9). *The FBI Relied on a Private Firm's Investigation of the DNC Hack—Which Makes the Agency Harder to Trust*. Retrieved from Slate.com: https://slate.com/technology/2017/05/the-fbi-is-harder-to-trust-on-the-dnc-hack-because-it-relied-on-crowdstrikes-analysis.html

Yochai Benkler, R. F. (2017, March 3). *Study: Breitbart-led right wing media ecosystem altered broader media agenda*. Retrieved from CJR.org: https://www.cjr.org/analysis/breitbart-media-trump-harvard-study.php

INDEX

ABC, 23, 24, 25, 35, 37, 98, 100

Alperovitch, Dmitri, 113

Annual Report of Economic Freedom, 3

Arpiao, Joe, 93

Assange, Julian, 114, 115

Attkisson, Sharyl, 35

Ayers, Bill, 31

Barr, Bill, 119

BBC, 1

Biden, Hunter, 74

Biden, Joe, 74

   Vice President Biden, 10, 74

Binney, Bill, 113

Boyle, Matthew, 42

Brazile, Donna, 115

Bruce, Tammy, 44

Bureau of Labor Statistics

   BLS, 28

Burke, Edmond, 18

Burr, Richard, 109

Bush, George W., 24

   GW Bush, 7

   President Bush, 24, 25, 26, 32

Byrd, Robert, 76

Carlin, John, 96

Carney, Jay, 35

CBO, 82

CBS, 23, 24, 25, 35, 37, 43

China, 3, 10, 11, 12, 13, 14, 20, 21, 46, 51, 85, 86, 133, 146

Clapper, James, 39, 96, 113

Clevenger, Ty, 116

Clinton Foundation, 66, 67, 68, 69

Clinton, Bill, 19, 44, 62

Clinton, Hillary, 5, 37, 47, 52, 62, 64, 67, 68, 69, 71, 91, 92, 93, 94, 97, 106, 110, 111, 115, 116, 120, 121, 123, 127, 132, 133

CNBC, 29, 34, 126

CNN, 16, 23, 30, 34, 35, 134

Cohen, Michael, 124

Columbia Journalism Review, 47, 49, 50, 54, 143

Comey, James, 39, 40, 91, 92, 93, 98, 102, 103, 104, 105, 107, 108, 109, 112, 116

Concord Management, 125, 128, 129, 130

Coulter, Ann, 26, 30

Crowdstrike, 74, 109, 111, 112, 113, 117, 118, 125

Deep State, 16, 38, 39, 41, 70, 74, 88, 91, 98, 100, 101, 102, 103, 105, 107, 109, 110, 118, 119, 130, 131, 132

Democrat, 5, 31, 36, 38, 41, 62, 67, 69, 71, 77, 115, 131, 133

Democrats, 16, 25, 31, 41, 42, 45, 47,
    50, 52, 60, 61, 62, 70, 71, 73, 74,
    75, 76, 102, 106, 107, 108, 111,
    117, 118, 119, 133, 136
Department of Justice, 31, 70, 71,
    72, 103
DOJ, 31, 38, 70, 71, 72, 73, 75, 93, 94,
    95, 96, 97, 100, 101, 103, 105,
    106, 107, 112, 118, 120, 124, 132
Dingle, John, 77
Dobbs, Lou, 99
Douglas, William O., 77

Facebook, 21, 42, 48, 49, 50, 51, 53,
    54, 55, 56, 57, 58, 120, 126, 127,
    142, 143, 144, 145
Falco, Nick, 98
Farrell, Chris, 99
Federal Reserve, 1
the Fed, 2, 9, 83, 84, 85, 86, 87,
    89, 90
Ferguson, 30
FISA, 39, 41, 70, 71, 72, 73, 95, 96, 97,
    100, 106, 118, 121
Flynn, General Mike, 101, 102, 105,
    106, 108, 121
Food Stamps, 2, 9

Gallup, 23, 24, 29, 35, 60, 61
Gates, Richard, 123
Grassley, Chuck, 103
Greenspan, Alan, 1
Gregory, David, 25

Halper, Stefan, 102
Harlan, Marshal, 78
Hoft, Jim, 19, 36, 42, 54, 142
Holder, Eric, 31
Horowitz, Michael, 71, 72

IC IG, 75, 76
ICANN, 46

Iraq, 19, 21, 24, 25, 26, 61
Jackson, Judge Amy, 122
Jefferson, Thomas, 19
Jones, Alex, 51
Judicial Watch, 99, 117

Krugman, Paul, 6

Levin, Mark, 79
Lewinsky, Monica, 19
Libya, 32, 33, 64
Lu Wei, 21

Mainstream Media, 36, 39, 41, 98,
    130, 133
Manafort, Paul, 122
Media
    Fourth Estate, 18, 19, 145
Media Research Center, 24, 37
Mifsud, Joseph, 102
Moseley, Virginia, 35
MSM, 6, 22, 23, 28, 30, 32, 33, 35, 36, 38,
    39, 41, 42, 54, 69, 74, 98, 100, 105,
    107, 115, 118, 125, 127, 134, 135, 143

IN GOD WE TRUST

MSNBC, 34
Mueller, Robert, 39, 40, 70, 73, 74, 97,
    102, 107, 108, 109, 114, 118, 119,
    120, 121, 122, 123, 124, 125, 126,
    127, 128, 129, 130, 131, 133

Naughton, John, 22
NBC, 21, 24, 25, 35, 37
New media, 42, 59
New York Times, 5, 6, 24, 28, 29, 34,
    35, 36, 48, 63, 67, 105, 134
Nides, Tom, 35
Nunes, Devin, 70, 71, 130

Obama, Barack
    Obama, 4, 5, 7, 8, 9, 10, 15, 23, 24,
        25, 26, 29, 31, 32, 33, 35, 36, 38,
        40, 42, 43, 44, 45, 46, 47, 58, 60,
        61, 62, 64, 74, 75, 81, 83, 89, 90,
        91, 93, 94, 95, 96, 97, 100, 101,
        103, 104, 105, 110, 113, 116, 117,
        121, 122, 124, 125, 132, 147
    Obama's Presidency, 5
    President Obama, 1
Oconus lures, 98
Ohr, Bruce, 72, 101
Ohr, Nellie, 72, 101

Page, Carter, 71, 95, 97, 100, 106, 118
Page, Lisa, 97, 117
Pai, Ajit, 45
Papadopoulos, George, 123
Pientka, Joe, 105

Pinedo, Richard, 124
Podesta, John, 116, 122
Powell, Jerome, 85, 86, 87, 89
Powell, Sidney, 101

Radio Free Europe, 19, 20, 21, 59
Ravel, Ann, 45
Reagan, Ronald, 7
Republicans, 34, 35, 60, 61, 62,
    71, 75, 108
Rhoades, Ben, 35, 36
Rhoades, David, 35
Rice, Susan, 104
Rich, Seth, 115, 116, 117
Rogers, Admiral Mike, 95
Roosevelt, Franklin D., 78
Rosenstein, Rod, 107, 119, 120
Rybicki, James, 116

Sanders, Bernie, 55, 115
Schiff, Adam, 69, 70, 71, 72, 75, 76
Sessions, Jeff, 106
Sherwood, Ben, 35
Sherwood-Randall, Dr. Elizabeth, 35
Steele, Christopher, 72
Stockman, David, 1
Stone, Roger, 124
Strzok, Peter, 97, 105, 117, 121

Tanner, Michael, 2
The DOW, 6, 7
The Gateway Pundit, 6, 10, 54, 55,
    57, 58, 142, 143, 144

TIME Magazine, 22

Truman, Harry, 78

Trump, Donald, 1, 6, 7, 38, 46, 55, 69, 72, 81, 93, 94, 100, 111, 125, 127, 132

President Trump, 5, 6, 7, 8, 9, 10, 11, 14, 15, 16, 37, 38, 39, 40, 41, 66, 74, 75, 81, 83, 85, 86, 88, 89, 90, 94, 95, 96, 97, 98, 99, 101, 102, 103, 104, 105, 106, 107, 108, 109, 117, 118, 119, 122, 125, 127, 130, 132, 133, 134, 136, 140

Trump Administration, 11, 73

Twitter, 21, 42, 48, 50, 51, 55, 98, 99, 100, 126

Unemployment, 15, 27

van der Zwan, Alex, 124

Walesa, Lech, 20

Wall Street Journal, 24

Washington Post, 23, 43, 105, 110, 134

Western Journal, 58

Wheeler, Tom, 45

WikiLeaks, 111, 114, 115, 116, 117, 123

Wilcox, Ella Wheeler, 44

Williams, Brian, 21

Woods, James, 51

Xi Jinping, 10

Yates, Sally, 104, 105, 121, 122

YouTube, 21, 53, 114

ABOUT THE AUTHOR

Joe Hoft loves the United States of America and the current President of the United States, Donald J. Trump. He shows this in the posts that he writes for his twin brother Jim at his website www.thegateway-pundit.com.

Joe has written articles that were national headlines at the *Drudge Report* and others that were tweeted by President Trump.

Joe is a financial, operational and IT professional with expertise in the financial services industry. He has worked for years in the Asia-Pacific region and lived in Hong Kong as a corporate executive for nearly a decade. Hoft has ten degrees or designations and has authored articles and reports published and prepared for various Board meetings, academic journals and major websites.

Joe has visited companies around the world in the US, Hong Kong, Singapore, Malaysia, China, Taiwan, Japan, Korea, India, Australia, New Zealand, Argentina, Canada, the UK, Spain, Portugal and South Africa. His skillset in identifying issues and offering suggestions, and his ability to see things that others don't, has benefited him throughout his career.

Joe is the author of *Falling Eagle—Rising Tigers*, a book about solutions for the US from the Asia Pacific region. He wrote this in the middle of the Obama Administration and offered working solutions to pressing problems in the US at that time.

Joe also is the author of *Loving, Blessing and Being Aware of God's Grace*. This book is a catalog of personal stories that teach lessons on how to live a content and grateful life no matter what comes your way.

Printed in Great Britain
by Amazon

56362373R00099

Printed in Great Britain
by Amazon